P   T
C   S

HEATHER
VOIGHT

PASSIONATE CRUSADERS

How Members of the U.S. War Refugee
Board Saved Jews and Altered American
Foreign Policy during World War II

973.917
VOIGHT, H

First published in 2015 by
Heather Voight

3 1257 02506 0152

Paperback ISBN: 978-0-9903052-0-0
eBook edition also available

http://www.heathervoight.com

Cover design by Jane Dixon-Smith
Typesetting by Chenile Keogh

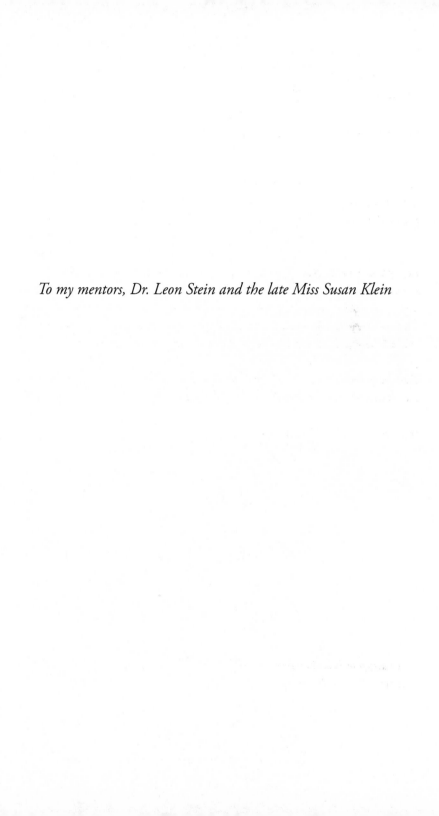

To my mentors, Dr. Leon Stein and the late Miss Susan Klein

Contents

Foreword

IN 1944, WHEN THE NAZI Holocaust against the European Jews continued unabated and when anti-Semitism in America reached its peak, a small number of non-Jews in the United States Treasury Department and some Jewish activists pressured the Roosevelt administration to rescue the persecuted Jews of Europe. These courageous men were able to rescue thousands of Jews and change both American behavior and international law.

Heather Voight's well-researched and timely study of the War Refugee Board tells their gripping story and adds new insights to this episode of World War II. It shows how at that time the State Department not only tried to prevent Jews from entering the United States, but also suppressed information about the Holocaust from the American news media and the larger public. A few good men were outraged.

Henry Morgenthau, John Pehle, Josiah DuBois, Randolph Paul, and Peter Bergson confronted the Roosevelt administration and threatened a scandal if the anti-Semitic behavior of the State Department under Breckinridge Long and the blind eye of the Roosevelt administration toward the State Department were allowed to continue. Roosevelt met with these men, gave way, and created the War Refugee Board in 1944. As a result thousands of Jews were rescued in Hungary and Rumania, and America set a new course in dealing with persecuted minorities in other lands.

As Heather Voight shows, this was too little and much too late but in its way the War Refugee Board changed history. From January 1944 onward the United States embarked on the course of a more active approach to helping the Jews of Europe. One of the most important findings of the book is the impact that the courageous men in the Treasury Department made on international law. They were able to pressure Herbert Pell of the War Crimes Commission to highlight the mass murder of civilians, thereby broadening the definition of war crimes, which came to be called crimes against humanity. This became a lasting precedent, as evidenced in the attitudes and actions taken in response to atrocities in Bosnia and Rwanda.

This study is fair to criticize the Roosevelt administration's inaction up until 1944, for the men in Treasury were also critical of the administration at the time. Still, the book also shows that the efforts of an honorable and courageous few can make small steps toward changing history. This detailed, well-told, and inspiring story will be of value to students of the Holocaust, American history, and human rights.

Leon Stein, PhD
Professor Emeritus of History, Roosevelt University and
Education Director Emeritus, Illinois Holocaust Museum
and Education Center

Preface

IN HIS RECENT BOOK, *FDR and the Jews*, author Richard Breitman states that "there is still a need for a thorough study of the War Refugee Board (WRB)."[1] The following pages comprise the first book ever written about the War Refugee Board and its members. Of course, this book does not exist in a vacuum; other authors have written articles about the Board and some have devoted chapters to the topic. In his 1980 article "Jewish Organizations and the Creation of the War Refugee Board," Monty Penkower describes the creation of the WRB. Penkower commends Treasury Department officials for their desire to save the remaining Jews of Europe in 1944. Their persistence revealed the State Department's reluctance, and sometimes outright refusal, to aid Jews during the Holocaust. Finally, members of the Treasury confronted President Franklin Roosevelt with the State's treachery.[2]

In the 1990s, the War Refugee Board received attention from more scholars. David Wyman devotes a section of his book *The Abandonment of the Jews* to the WRB, in which he examines the Board's activities in various countries and gives credit to its members for their efforts to save lives. Wyman also cites some of the primary material on the Board, including documents from the FDR library. Another author, Ariel Hurwitz, examines FDR's motives for creating

---

1 Richard Breitman and Allan J. Lichtman, *FDR and the Jews* (Cambridge, MA: Harvard University Press, 2013), 402, note 60.

2 Monty Penkower, "Jewish Organizations and the Creation of the U.S. War Refugee Board," *The Annals of the American Academy of Political and Social Science* 450, no. 1: 122–139, July 1980 [journal online]; downloaded from http://www.jstor.org/stable/1042563; Internet; accessed 6 March 2014.

the WRB in his 1991 article "The Struggle Over the Creation of the War Refugee Board." Specifically, Hurwitz argues that the Treasury Department's Report to the President was more influential in the Board's creation than the congressional resolution that recommended a new rescue agency.[3] Although the aforementioned studies provide a good introduction to the War Refugee Board, they do not tell the whole story. Penkower explains how and why the Board was created, but does not analyze the Board's rescue and relief efforts, except to say that the Board came into existence too late to accomplish much. Hurwitz provides a perspective on why FDR created the Board but also concludes his study by stating that the Board had little success in saving lives. Wyman provides a more in-depth study of the Board; however, he agrees with the other authors' assessment that the WRB was created far too late to be effective.

Due to space constraints, articles and book chapters on a topic like the War Refugee Board cannot deal with all of the relevant documents. For example, in contrast to Penkower's article, which primarily cites the diaries of Treasury Secretary Henry Morgenthau, this book is the culmination of years of researching the War Refugee Board's papers. Some of the documents cited in this book came from the microfilm collections of universities and of the Library of Congress, while others were discovered during my visit to the Franklin D. Roosevelt Presidential Library and Museum in Hyde Park, New York.

The purpose of all this research was not to point out that the FDR administration or the Allies failed to help Jews, nor is it to criticize the WRB for its shortcomings. Other authors have already focused on the failure of the Allies in general and of the WRB in particular to rescue Jews. The Board was comprised of human beings and was therefore imperfect. This book does not skim over the faults of WRB members or the FDR administration, but its purpose is

---

3   Ariel Hurwitz, "The Struggle Over the Creation of the War Refugee Board," *Holocaust and Genocide Studies* 6, no.1: 17–31, 1991 [journal online]; downloaded from http://hgs.oxfordjournals.org; Internet; accessed 20 March 2014.

not to find fault. Instead, I sought to find out what, if anything, the Board accomplished. To what extent did it carry out its mission, stated in the executive order that created the Board, to "develop plans for rescue, transportation, maintenance and relief of the victims of enemy oppression"?[4] What methods did the Board employ to aid Jews? How many Jews were aided by the WRB? Do the actions of the Board and its members still influence how the United States responds to genocide in the twenty-first century?

In addition to answering the above questions through my research, I also set out to write this book in a style that would be accessible to every American. Yehuda Bauer, the leading Israeli historian of the Holocaust, states in the *History of the Holocaust* that the establishment of the War Refugee Board was "a major event in the history of the war."[5] This is not a topic that deserves to languish in obscurity. Unfortunately many Americans still know nothing about the Board or the actions of its members. If the following pages introduce even one person to the attempts of the Board to save the Jews, then the years it took to produce them were worthwhile.

---

4 Franklin D. Roosevelt, Executive Order No. 9417, 22 January 1944, Papers of the War Refugee Board, ed. Robert Lester, (Bethesda, MD: UPA collection from LexisNexis, 2002–6).

5 Yehuda Bauer, *A History of the Holocaust* (Danbury, CT: Franklin Watts, 1982), 318.

CHAPTER ONE

A Plan of Inaction: The United States Government's Track Record on Jewish Rescue, 1941–43

On a Sunday afternoon in January 1944, three men from the Treasury Department waited in the Oval Office to meet with President Franklin D. Roosevelt. Although their backgrounds, ages, and religions differed, each shared one goal that day. They hoped to save as many Jews as possible in Nazi-occupied Europe by securing FDR's support for a new rescue agency. The War Refugee Board, as the agency was eventually called, did help Jews, but it also accomplished something its founders never realized during their lifetimes. Through their actions, members of the Board permanently altered American foreign and immigration policy. This is the story of the War Refugee Board and its employees. Though not infallible, they did whatever they could to save the lives of people whom they had never met and influenced America's response to future genocides.

To understand why President Roosevelt agreed to create the War Refugee Board when he did, his actions on human rights issues prior to January 1944 must be examined. Long before the members of the Treasury met with FDR to discuss the need for a new rescue agency, FDR demonstrated his willingness to bend under political and public pressure. One example of this occurred between FDR and the Brotherhood of Sleeping Car Porters (BSCP). Although many unemployed white workers succeeded in obtaining defense industry jobs during 1940, black workers struggled to find work.

By October 1940 the unemployment rate for whites had fallen to 13 percent, but unemployment among blacks had declined by only one-tenth of 1 percent.[1] Even when blacks found employment, they almost always worked in service positions that paid little, such as train car porters.

The problems of African American workers did not interest FDR until black leaders from the Brotherhood of Sleeping Car Porters and the National Association for the Advancement of Colored People (NAACP) presented him with an ultimatum. Weary of setting up meetings with government officials who failed to act on their promises, BSCP leader A. Philip Randolph and NAACP leader Walter White joined forces to support a mass march of African Americans at the Lincoln Memorial on July 1, 1941. When FDR heard about the planned march, he invited Randolph and White to meet him at the White House. During the meeting, Randolph stressed that blacks wanted "something tangible, definite, positive, and affirmative."[2] What they wanted was an executive order stating that African Americans would not face discrimination when they applied for government or defense jobs. If the president did not agree to their request, 100,000 African Americans from across the country would march on Washington. Faced with a possible mass demonstration practically at his front door, FDR decided to issue Executive Order 8802. The order stated, "There shall be no discrimination in the employment of workers in defense industries or government because of race, creed, color, or national origin."[3]

In 1942 FDR was again influenced by outside forces, this time in his treatment of Japanese Americans. He signed an executive order that authorized the removal of Japanese American citizens from their homes and placed them in internment camps. Indifferent to the suffering of a people he considered inferior, FDR was vulnerable to political pressure regarding Japanese Americans. Later, he would

---

1   Beth Tompkins Bates, *Pullman Porters and the Rise of Protest Politics in Black America 1925–1945* (Chapel Hill, NC: University of North Carolina Press, 2001), 151.
2   Ibid., 158.
3   Ibid., 160.

be vulnerable to similar pressure regarding Jews. By 1942 anti-Japanese sentiment in America was no longer a new issue. For example, in 1940 *Life* magazine warned its readers of potentially subversive activity among Japanese Americans.[4] White farmers and shop owners on the Pacific coast resented the success of their Japanese American counterparts. Even FDR was not immune to prejudice. As early as the 1920s, FDR wrote articles that described Japanese immigrants as being of "oriental blood" and therefore unable to fully assimilate into American society.[5] To FDR, Japanese immigrants represented their home country regardless of how long they had been in the United States. As president, FDR requested reports on the loyalty of Japanese Americans to the US from the FBI and secret agents from other organizations. Although these reports described them as pro-American, FDR "personally supervised a secret campaign to guard against sabotage and prepare for the summary arrest of [Japanese American] suspects."[6]

After the Japanese attack on Pearl Harbor, public hostility toward Japanese Americans dramatically increased. To white farmers and business owners in states like California, Pearl Harbor presented the perfect opportunity to force their Japanese American competition out of the area. By early 1942 FDR and other government officials were receiving about 200 letters per week advocating the evacuation of Japanese Americans from the Pacific coast to the interior of the country.[7] California's government officials, reporters, and even United States senators from other states feared that Japanese Americans would help Japan invade the West Coast if they were not evacuated. War Department officials, including Secretary of War Henry Stimson and Assistant Secretary John McCloy, also supported evacuation. The Japanese were temporarily winning the war in the Pacific, and an invasion of the West Coast seemed possible. Under

---

4   Greg Robinson, *By Order of the President: FDR and the Internment of Japanese Americans* (Cambridge, MA: Harvard University Press, 2001), 87.

5   Ibid., 41.

6   Ibid., 72.

7   Ibid., 102.

pressure from public opinion, government officials, and his own War Department, an already suspicious FDR signed the executive order that resulted in the deportation of over 100,000 American citizens from the Pacific coast to internment camps.[8] FDR's response to political and public opinions on human rights issues in the early 1940s foreshadowed his eventual creation of a new rescue agency for European Jews. However, the War Refugee Board was not created until most of Europe's Jews had been murdered.

When the persecution of Jews first began in Germany, FDR showed some signs of sympathy for them. The United States government gave European Jews reason to hope that it might help them in the aftermath of November 9, 1938, known as Kristallnacht (the Night of Broken Glass), when the Nazis burned Jewish homes and synagogues and arrested thousands of Jews and put them in prison camps.[9] Defenders of President Roosevelt's reputation are quick to claim that his response to Kristallnacht was the strongest of any democratic leader. They cite the fact that FDR extended visitor's visas for the 12,000 Jews already in the United States. He also said in a press conference that he could "scarcely believe that such things could occur in a twentieth-century civilization" and he recalled the United States ambassador to Germany.[10] Although it is true that neither France nor Britain recalled their ambassadors, Britain took more significant action than the US in the aftermath of Kristallnacht by admitting 10,000 German Jewish refugee children. In addition, 14,000 German Jewish women were admitted as cooks and nannies.[11]

However, thousands more Jews lining up at United States

8   Ibid., 108.

9   Saul Friedman, *No Haven for the Oppressed* (Detroit: Wayne State University Press, 1973), 73.

10   Franklin D. Roosevelt, draft statement by the President, 15 November 1938; Folder: Diplomatic Correspondence, Germany 1933–1938; President's Secretary's Files; Papers of the War Refugee Board; Franklin D. Roosevelt Library, Hyde Park, NY.

11   Rafael Medoff, "Reexamining FDR's Response to Kristallnacht," *Tablet Magazine*, 4 November 2014; http://tabletmag.com/scroll/186766/reexamining-fdrs-response-to-kristallnacht.

consulates in Europe hoping to gain entry to the US were less fortunate. Among these were the parents of Kurt Klein. Kurt and his siblings had immigrated to America from Waldorf, Germany, in the hope that they could make enough money to send for their parents.[12] Before Kurt's mother and father could pack their bags, however, they had to overcome two major obstacles. The first was the restrictive immigration policy of the United States. The second was the hostility of State Department officials toward immigrants, especially Jews.

In 1924 Congress enacted strict immigration laws. During the Great Depression, these laws remained in effect. The maximum number of people who were permitted to immigrate to the US in 1929 was 153,774—considerably fewer than the 900,000 maximum allowed at the start of the century.[13] The countries that were home to the largest number of potential immigrants were assigned small quotas. For example, in 1929 the quota for German immigrants was 26,000, and even this figure was not reached.[14] In contrast, countries with few people clamoring to leave received much higher quotas. Britain and Ireland had an annual quota of 83,575, much of which remained unused.[15]

At a time when jobs were scarce and many Americans didn't have enough money to support themselves, some immigration restrictions were understandable. What is more difficult to understand is the fact that these immigration laws remained in place despite improvement in the economy. Although the US economy was not booming in 1938, it was in better shape than it had been a decade earlier. Why did the United States cling to such strict immigration laws while the

---

12   Kurt Klein, interview by Marty Ostrow, video recording, 1992, *America and the Holocaust: Deceit and Indifference*. 60 min., PBS, 1993.

13   Arthur D. Morse, *While Six Million Died* (Woodstock, NY: Ace Publishing Co., 1983), 134.

14   Herbert Hoover, Proclamation 1872—Limiting the Immigration of Aliens into the United States on the Basis of National Origin, 22 March 1929. Online by Gerhard Peters and John T. Woolley, *The American Presidency Project*. http://www.presidency.ucsb.edu

15   Ibid.

Jews of Europe faced disease, starvation, and possible death in ghettos?

Prior to the establishment of the death camps in October 1941, emigration of Jews was permitted in most Nazi-occupied territories. Hitler personally expressed his willingness to send Jews to Western democracies and thus be rid of them.[16] Yet the State Department strengthened the laws rather than relaxing them.

Kurt Klein's father wrote in December 1938 that he and Kurt's mother had to wait for an appointment just to apply for a visa. Their waiting number indicated there were 22,344 cases ahead of them.[17] Unless State changed its policies, the Klein family would never be reunited.

The appointment of Breckinridge Long as assistant secretary of state ensured that State's hostility toward immigration continued. Long and FDR became friends early in FDR's political career. After Germany invaded Poland, FDR appointed his old friend to the position of assistant secretary of state, which put him in charge of refugee matters.[18] Long oversaw the divisions for relief, transportation, and visas for immigrants. He not only showed a willingness to follow the current immigration laws, but also let it be known that he wanted even fewer immigrants admitted to the United States. In a memo to State Department officials, Long wrote, "We can delay and effectively stop for a temporary period of indefinite length the number of immigrants into the United States. We could do this by simply advising our consuls, to put every obstacle in the way ... which would postpone and postpone and postpone the granting of visas."[19] The consuls followed Long's instructions, and FDR avoided the refugee issue. At the

16 Morse, 204.
17 Kurt Klein, interview by Marty Ostrow. *America and the Holocaust.*
18 Fred L. Israel, introduction to *The War Diary of Breckinridge Long*, by Breckinridge Long (Lincoln, NE: University of Nebraska Press, 1966), xxiv.
19 Memo from Assistant Secretary of State Breckinridge Long to State Department Officials, June 26, 1940. Online by PBS, *America and the Holocaust*, www.pbs.org

end of 1940 Kurt Klein's father wrote that even visa applications that had been approved would be reassessed.[20]

Long's motives for limiting immigration became a topic of debate among his contemporaries. Some saw anti-Semitism behind the State Department's inaction on Jewish immigration. Treasury Department official Edward Bernstein stated there was a "clear anti-Semitic environment" in the State Department.[21] John Pehle, Treasury Department official and future director of the War Refugee Board, stopped short of calling State Department employees anti-Semitic, though he acknowledged that refugee matters "tended to be pushed to the side."[22] Long offered a different though erroneous explanation. He stated in his diary that he feared refugees might be Nazi agents incognito—an idea he subsequently presented to FDR.[23] Even if Long believed his spy theory, the record indicates that only one enemy agent entered the United States as a refugee, and the refugee was not Jewish.[24]

Whatever Long's motives, he was not the only government official who sought to deter refugees from entering the country. He received considerable aid from an isolationist Congress. On June 20, 1941 the Bloom-Van Nuys Bill (also known as the relative rule) was passed. Under this bill, refugees with relatives in Nazi-occupied territory could be rejected because of State's claims that Nazis held relatives hostage to coerce refugees into becoming Nazi agents.[25] Since most Jews had relatives in Nazi-held territories, the relative rule made it extremely difficult for them to enter the US.

The Bloom-Van Nuys Bill also added to the difficulty by creating further levels of bureaucracy for an applicant to navigate

---

20   Kurt Klein, interview by Marty Ostrow, *America and the Holocaust.*
21   Rafael Medoff, *Blowing the Whistle on Genocide* (West Lafayette, IN: Purdue University Press, 2009), 18.
22   John Pehle, interview by Marty Ostrow, 1992, *America and the Holocaust.*
23   Breckinridge Long, *The War Diary of Breckinridge Long: Selections from the Years 1939–1944,* comp. and ed. Fred L. Israel (Lincoln, NE: University of Nebraska Press, 1966), 213.
24   Morse, 39.
25   Friedman, 122.

before a visa was approved. First, US consuls reviewed applications. Their decisions were then confirmed or rejected by a committee of members from State, Navy, Army, Justice, and FBI departments. Unsuccessful applicants could appeal to a special committee of review, then to a board of appeals, and finally to the Secretary of State.[26] Most discovered the futility of appealing, since by then they or the relatives for whom they sought visas had been transported to a concentration camp, never to be heard from again. Thanks to his efforts and those of his siblings, Kurt Klein received a notice in November 1942 from the State Department approving his parents' visas. But the Department's letter came two and a half months after his parents' deportation to an unknown destination in Eastern Europe.[27]

The Bloom-Van Nuys Bill was used to turn away thousands of potential immigrants and may have been a factor in Hitler's decision to halt legal emigration. Another, much larger, factor was America's entry into World War II in 1941. America's involvement in the war sped up the Holocaust. By this time Hitler had decided to cut all ties to the West and to exterminate the Jews. One reason he did this was because the Western democracies consistently refused to take in more Jews. Hitler also believed, based on the few Jews working in the Roosevelt administration, that Jews controlled the United States government. Legal emigration from Nazi territories ended, making State's claim that the Nazis wanted to send in Jewish spies moot.

Early in the war most Americans agreed with the actions of their government. Anti-Semitism was commonplace among the American public. Between 1940 and 1941, public opinion surveys showed that 17–20 percent of Americans thought Jews were a threat to the United States, making them more unpopular than Germans or blacks.[28] Anti-Semitism increased during the war and only declined when it was nearly over.[29] FDR, who had already shown

---

26 Ibid.
27 Kurt Klein, interview by Marty Ostrow, *America and the Holocaust.*
28 Yehuda Bauer, *A History of the Holocaust* (Danbury, CT: Franklin Watts, 1982), 297.
29 Ibid.

he could be influenced by public opinion where minorities were concerned, showed minimal interest in Europe's Jews until public opinion began to change in late 1943 and early 1944. During 1943 the State Department showed no sign of relaxing its iron grip on visa procedures. In January of that year the State Department literally added a few more feet to the already staggering length of red tape visa applicants endured by implementing a 4-foot long form. This form, known as Form BC, required, among other stipulations, that the applicant list any relatives he or she had in other countries in accordance with the relative rule, sign a proclamation that he or she was not a communist, and provide two letters of reference from American citizens who vouched for the character and financial stability of the applicant.[30] Thanks to Form BC and the relative rule, the State Department turned away many refugees. From late 1941 until early 1945, just 10 percent of the already tiny quotas from Axis-controlled countries were filled.[31] Long and other government officials got what they wanted; immigration from Nazi-occupied countries nearly came to a halt, leaving Jews to fend for themselves against their persecutors.

In late 1942 the State Department had a public relations issue on its hands. In addition to limiting immigration, State also limited the flow of information on the persecution of the Jews. Its officials claimed that reports of such terrible acts were unreliable, at least until Rabbi Stephen Wise leaked information he had received from Europe to the public.[32] Wise was a respected member of the Jewish community and well known for his honesty. Once his name was associated with reports of atrocities, he successfully organized forty rallies across the country calling for revised immigration procedures.[33]

---

30   Visa Application of the U.S. State Department, Visa Division, January 1943. Online by PBS, *America and the Holocaust*, www.pbs.org

31   Medoff, *Blowing the Whistle*, 4.

32   Memorandum on Bermuda Conference on the refugee problem, April 1943, Papers of the War Refugee Board, ed. Robert Lester (Bethesda, MD: UPA collection from LexisNexis, 2002–6).

33   *America and the Holocaust*, prod. Marty Ostrow.

During the 1940s, a recent Jewish immigrant named Peter Bergson heard Wise's report about Nazi atrocities. Furious that the American press had buried the information on the inside pages of newspapers, Bergson garnered support from political leaders and artists to get the word out about the Holocaust. These men and women, known as the Bergson group, bought full-page ad space in the *New York Times* as well as other major US newspapers like the *Washington Post*. After the government confirmed the news of Jewish extermination, Bergson ran an ad in the *New York Times* under the headline ACTION—NOT PITY.[34] The Bergson group wanted the public to know that the government could still save some Jews if it wished.

In an effort to make the ads as effective as possible, Bergson contacted Ben Hecht, a famous Jewish screenwriter and journalist, who wrote of his frustration that most American Jews refused to speak out against the Holocaust.[35] One of Hecht's most disturbing ads appeared in the *New York Times* on September 14, 1943. Hecht wrote "The Ballad of the Doomed Jews of Europe," beginning with the stanza:

> *Four million Jews waiting for death*
> *Oh hang and burn but—quiet, Jews!*
> *Don't be bothersome; save your breath*
> *The world is busy with other news.*[36]

The world was indeed more concerned with "other news," at least until the ads started to shake things up.

Congressman Will Rogers, Jr. commented in an interview years later that "the Ben Hecht ads did more than any other single event to stimulate Americans that wanted to save Jews to take action."[37] The public no longer had an excuse to simply pity the Jews. People

---

34   "Action—Not Pity," *New York Times*, 8 February 1943. Reprinted in David Wyman, *A Race Against Death: Peter Bergson, America, and the Holocaust.* (New York: The New Press, 2002).

35   Wyman, *A Race Against Death*, 25.

36   Ben Hecht, "Ballad of the Doomed Jews of Europe," *New York Times*, 14 September 1943. Reprinted in David Wyman, *A Race Against Death*.

37   Will Rogers, Jr., interview by Marty Ostrow, 1993, *America and the Holocaust*.

could take action by supporting the Bergson group's Emergency Committee to Save the Jewish People of Europe. Bergson gave people the opportunity to contribute money to fund publicity efforts or volunteer their time.

Bergson used other means besides the press to bring attention to the plight of Europe's Jews. In addition to creating ads, Bergson used his relationship with Hecht to produce a dramatic pageant about the murder of the Jews, called *We Will Never Die*.[38] The pageant featured prominent actors who donated their time to bring knowledge of the Holocaust directly to the public. Actors Paul Muni, Edward G. Robinson, and Stella Adler starred in the show, with Moss Hart as the director. The actors performed the show twice on March 9, 1943 in Madison Square Garden.[39] Americans who eagerly attended the shows to see their favorite actors left with an awareness of Jewish history and the ongoing persecution of the Jews. In addition to Madison Square Garden, the pageant played to packed houses in Washington, DC, Philadelphia, Chicago, Boston, and Los Angeles.[40]

Thanks to the actions of men like Bergson, letters poured into the State Department and the White House demanding that the United States government condemn Jewish persecution. The public also wanted the British and Americans to take action to help the Jews. Fortunately, the British government, also responding to public pressure, had an idea. Britain proposed that both countries hold a conference to discuss the number of visas that each country would issue to refugees.[41] Despite the mail both State and the president received on the plight of Europe's Jews, the United States government took its time responding to Britain's request for a meeting. Though the British came up with the idea in February 1943, State stalled until April before appointing delegates to the conference.[42]

---

38 Wyman, *A Race Against Death*, 34–5.
39 Ibid.
40 Ibid.
41 Memorandum on Bermuda Conference on the refugee problem, April 1943, Papers of the War Refugee Board.
42 Ibid.

The conference was to take place in Bermuda, but even at that distance State assumed control over the US delegates. State sent a memorandum to each delegate, containing instructions as to what they could not do during the conference. Given the long list of forbidden topics, it would have been easier to list what was permitted to be discussed. For example, delegates were not allowed to specifically mention Jews in their discussions because that might give the Axis powers the idea that the war was being fought for the Jews.[43]

Since nothing had been done for the Jews to date, it is unclear why the Nazis would worry about the United States' sudden affection for them. Another topic delegates were forbidden to mention was US immigration laws. State's memo stated, "It should be borne in mind that the United States immigration laws are fixed by Congress and *are extremely liberal as they stand* [my italics]."[44] As mentioned earlier in this chapter, the immigration laws were strict to begin with and the State Department refused even more immigrants who could have entered under the law. Essentially, the State Department sent delegates to Bermuda with instructions to accomplish nothing whatsoever.

When the conference finally convened, the United States delegates discovered that the British government was as unmotivated as their own to help Europe's Jews. In particular, the British, who controlled Palestine, refused to discuss opening the region to additional immigrants. Conference records indicate that "various possibilities for [re]locating refugees, and the problems connected with each were discussed at some length, but without any definite conclusion being reached."[45] With the exception of American delegate and Congressman Sol Bloom, no delegate from either country wanted to negotiate with Hitler for Jewish lives, because they assumed he would expect favors in return.[46] Of course the British and Americans

---

43 Ibid.
44 Ibid.
45 Ibid.
46 Ibid.

could not know that with any certainty unless they asked, which they did not.

Following the conference, the delegates made their recommendations to their respective countries. The recommendations confirmed that the US and Britain had no plans to save the Jews. Both governments sought to pass the refugee problem on to other countries rather than take in more immigrants themselves. According to the report, the British and Americans planned to send proposals to Latin American countries, Portugal and to other neutral governments.[47] Apparently no one thought to ask what motivation other governments would have to open their doors, if the US and Britain did not want refugees. Perhaps the question was not asked because the answer did not matter to two of the world's greatest democracies. All either country wanted was to keep immigrants out of their backyards. Avoiding the judgment of history and those who study it proved more difficult.

---

47   *Report to the Governments of the United Kingdom and the United States from their Delegates to the Conference on the Refugee Problem Held at Bermuda*, April 19–29, 1943, Summary of Recommendations, Chapter VII, Papers of the War Refugee Board.

CHAPTER TWO

A Call to Action: The Treasury Department's Report on Jewish Rescue

UNTIL MID-1943 IT SEEMED that the State Department would hold sway over refugee matters for the duration of FDR's presidency. State officials had already succeeded in blocking immigrants from coming to the United States on the pretense that they would somehow endanger the country. Even from a distance, State made certain that the Bermuda Conference would accomplish nothing, by issuing strict instructions to the American delegates. Yet the State Department soon discovered that it could not control the press or the actions of other government departments.

Once the results of the Bermuda Conference became public, Peter Bergson again used the press to influence public opinion. A full-page ad in the *New York Times* proclaimed, "To 5,000,000 Jews in the Nazi Death-Trap Bermuda was a Cruel Mockery When will the United Nations Establish an Agency to Deal with the Problem of Hitler's Extermination of a Whole People?"[1] While the Bergson group protested the failure of the Allies to help the Jews, the failure of the State Department to act on the rescue of Jewish refugees came to the attention of the United States Treasury. The evidence that Treasury members uncovered led FDR to consider the Bergson group's call for a new rescue agency.

Early in the year the State Department confirmed its determination to abandon the Jews even when rescue could be accomplished

---

1   "To 5,000,000 Jews in the Nazi Death-Trap," *New York Times*, 4 May 1943. Reprinted in David Wyman, *A Race Against Death*.

with minimal risk. On February 10, 1943, Gerhart Riegner, the Swiss Secretary of the World Jewish Congress, told State that the Rumanian government would allow 70,000 Jews to emigrate at the cost of 20,000 lei ($50 each).[2] In 1943 Rumania was a Nazi-controlled territory. Riegner suggested that the Allied funds to support the refugees be placed in blocked accounts in Switzerland, thus preventing the Nazis from accessing them.[3] With the Axis powers prevented from receiving Allied currency, Riegner must have felt sure of the State Department's approval.

One advantage of Riegner's plan was that the State Department could not make a final decision regarding the transfer of funds without requesting a license from the Treasury Department, which had recently altered its licensing policy. Earlier in the war, Treasury had refused requests from Jewish groups to license communications within enemy territory. Treasury Department officials felt blocking communications with the enemy was the best policy during a war. Unlike State, however, which did not change its policies unless forced to do so, Treasury officials later decided that some licenses could be safely issued provided the Nazis had no opportunity to obtain hard currency as a result.[4]

Riegner's plan stalled not because Treasury refused the license but because State never bothered to send a request to the Treasury Department. Instead, Secretary of the Treasury Henry Morgenthau heard about the plan during a July meeting with representatives of the American Jewish Congress (AJC). As they pleaded for the lives of Rumanian Jews, Morgenthau assured them that the Treasury was "fully sympathetic to the proposal."[5] After a conference with the State Department, Treasury Department officials approved the necessary license in just twenty-four hours. Yet State continued to

---

2   Friedman, 150.

3   David Wyman, *The Abandonment of the Jews* (New York: The New Press, 1984), 179.

4   John Pehle on the Conflict between the Treasury and State Department, interview transcript online by PBS, *America and the Holocaust*. www.pbs.org

5   John Morton Blum, *From the Morgenthau Diaries: Years of War 1941–1945* (Boston: Houghton Mifflin Co., 1967), 211.

procrastinate. State refused to give permission to its representative in Switzerland, Leland Harrison, to release the funds, despite Harrison's repeated requests for instruction.[6] While the lives of Rumanian Jews hung in the balance, State still had not replied to Harrison three months after Morgenthau's meeting with the AJC.

In response to State's inaction, John Pehle, head of the Foreign Funds Division of the Treasury, noted that State's cables to Harrison were "full of remarks like the *Treasury* wants this, the *Treasury* desires you to do this ... And Harrison, unless he is a dumbbell, can see through that, that State is in effect saying this is what the *Treasury* wants you to do [my italics]."[7] Pehle realized that the State Department, by refusing to give Harrison a direct order, intentionally stalled the license.

The State Department's procrastination was compounded by a cooperative agreement between State and the British government. Under the agreement, the release of US funds for the rescue of Jews also had to be cleared by the British. State undoubtedly recalled the negative attitude the British displayed toward Jewish immigrants at the Bermuda Conference and viewed the agreement as an excuse to refuse to aid refugees. As of December 15, 1943, the British Foreign Office remained concerned with "the difficulties of disposing of any considerable number of Jews should they be rescued."[8] Although the British stated their position more bluntly, the Foreign Office and the US State Department both saw Jews as garbage that needed to be disposed of elsewhere. In addition the British stated that it would be "almost if not quite impossible to deal with anything like the number of 70,000 refugees whose rescue is envisaged by the Riegner plan."[9] Interestingly, no one asked the British to take in all 70,000 refugees. If the world's greatest democracies had showed any interest in the plan, they could have asked other countries to find havens for

---

6   Ibid., 220.

7   Ibid., 213.

8   Telegram from American ambassador to Britain to US secretary of state, 15 December 1943, Papers of the War Refugee Board.

9   Ibid.

Jews. Instead, the number 70,000 was used as a convenient excuse for the British to refuse any number of refugees. By agreeing to wait for the reluctant British to approve the Treasury's license, State effectively doomed Rumanian Jews.

Although Morgenthau, Pehle, and others in the Treasury Department agreed that State's failure to act on the Riegner plan was inexcusable, they disagreed on what the Treasury Department should do. Some in Treasury wanted to confront FDR directly. Oscar Cox of the Foreign Economic Administration thought the president needed "a driving force that brings the viewpoint before the neutral countries, sees to it that the proper personnel is set up, sees to it that there is no defect in financing."[10] Only a rescue agency unencumbered by State Department red tape could accomplish Cox's goals. Though Morgenthau thought a new rescue agency might help, he still hoped to persuade State Department officials to change their policies.

Morgenthau found himself in a difficult position for two reasons. First, according to his daughter, he felt that he had to act as an American rather than as an American Jew if he wanted his opinions to be taken seriously.[11] Anti-Semitism was prevalent in the 1940s, and even though FDR hired Jews to his administration, he rarely ignored public opinion completely. Second, Morgenthau had a close personal relationship with the president that he did not wish to jeopardize by taking up a cause FDR disliked.

Morgenthau and Roosevelt met as neighbors in New York and soon became friends. After Roosevelt was elected Governor of New York, he appointed Morgenthau as State Commissioner of Conservation. During FDR's presidency, Morgenthau received another political appointment from his old friend. This time Morgenthau served as Secretary of the Treasury, which made him the only person of Jewish descent in FDR's cabinet. Even when the two friends disagreed over parts of Roosevelt's New Deal, Morgenthau

---

10   Blum, 217.
11   Joan Morgenthau on her father's relationship with the president, interview transcript online by PBS, *America and the Holocaust*, www.pbs.org

always supported FDR's decisions. In the late 1930s Morgenthau brought up possible havens for German Jews, but for the most part he did not pester FDR on immigration.[12]

In 1944 Morgenthau still hesitated to antagonize his friend. Instead, Morgenthau decided to take the information that the Treasury uncovered about State officials to Secretary of State Cordell Hull. He believed that Hull was a decent person whose good intentions had been subverted by his subordinates, including Breckinridge Long.[13]

When he met with Hull, Morgenthau discovered that Hull had already sent a response to the British. The secretary's cable made clear that the State Department disagreed with the attitude of the British government toward Rumanian refugees.[14] Under the circumstances, Morgenthau did not bring up the possibility of a separate rescue agency. Instead, an elated Morgenthau rushed back to the Treasury Department to tell his colleagues that Hull had taken care of the refugee crisis after all.[15] Although not all of his colleagues believed in Hull's ability to handle the refugee crisis, for the time being Morgenthau was satisfied with the State Department's response.

Harrison finally delivered the license to Riegner on December 23, 1943, about eleven months after Riegner had first contacted the State Department about the rescue of Rumanian Jews.[16] Unfortunately the Nazis did not suffer from the same bureaucratic inefficiencies as the State Department. By the time Riegner received his license, most of the Jews he had hoped to save had already been exterminated.[17] While Treasury officials, including Morgenthau, lamented State's slow response to the Riegner plan, they moved even closer to the discovery of another example of State Department sabotage: the

---

12   United States Holocaust Memorial Museum. "Henry Morgenthau." *Holocaust Encyclopedia.* http://www.ushmm.org

13   Blum, 218.

14   Paraphrase of telegram sent to London from secretary of state, 18 December 1943, Papers of the War Refugee Board.

15   Medoff, *Blowing the Whistle*, 30.

16   Blum, 220.

17   Friedman, 151.

deliberate suppression of information about the Holocaust. From mid-1942 to 1943 Riegner attempted to supply the Allied governments with information about the Final Solution. Riegner was the reliable source referred to in Chapter One whose message about Jewish extermination caused the British and American governments to hold the Bermuda Conference. The American Legation in Switzerland transmitted Riegner's first message on August 11, 1942. It referred to a conversation between Riegner and a German informant.[18] The telegram read, in Riegner's own words, "informer reported to have close connections with highest German authorities who has previously generally reliable reports."[19] Unsurprisingly the State Department refused to believe the "fantastic" allegations in Riegner's cable and ignored Riegner's request to send the information on to Rabbi Stephen Wise in New York.[20] Granted, since nothing like the Holocaust had occurred before, a rational person might wait for confirmation of Riegner's information.

If State wanted verification, however, it did not have to wait long. In late September the American consul in Geneva passed along two letters sent to Switzerland by a Jew in the Warsaw ghetto. Certain key words were written in Hebrew to circumvent Nazi censorship. One letter stated, "I spoke to Mr. Jaeger [the Germans]. He told me that he will invite all relatives of the family Achenu [the Jews] … from Warsaw to his mansion 'Kewer' [tomb]. Uncle Gerusch [deportation] also works in Warsaw … My friend Miso [death] now works with him."[21] This letter confirmed that deportation and death were already commonplace for European Jews. If State Department officials did not want to take the Jews' word for their sufferings, they had information from yet another source. In November Dr. Carl Burckhardt, a high

18   Yehuda Bauer, *Rethinking the Holocaust* (New Haven, CT: Yale University Press, 2001), 219.

19   Telegram received from Bern, 11 August 1942 by secretary of state, Washington, DC, online by PBS, *America and the Holocaust*, www.pbs.org

20   Morse, 14.

21   Varian Fry, "The Massacre of the Jews," *New Republic*, 21 December 1942. Reprinted in Robert Abzug, *America Views the Holocaust 1933–1945 A Brief Documentary History* (Boston: Bedford/St. Martin's, 1999), 130.

official of the International Red Cross, warned the American consul in Geneva that Hitler had ordered the annihilation of the Jews.[22] State now had the proof it had demanded to make the news of the Holocaust public, but its members needed to release the information. Instead, they kept the knowledge to themselves.

Although the Riegner report had been confirmed two months earlier, the State Department still had not published Riegner's message in January 1943. Stephen Wise was informed of the cable by the British and had already alerted the public when Minister Harrison transmitted a new cable, Number 482, containing a report from Riegner about the worsening plight of Jews in Europe. The new telegram no longer suggested that the Jews would be exterminated at a later date. Instead, Riegner stated that Germans were killing Polish Jews at the rate of 6,000 per day.[23] Meanwhile, Rumanian Jews were starving to death. The cable represented a turning point in Holocaust history because it led to the State Department's decision to block information on the extermination of the Jews. The American Legation's telegram prompted one from State to Harrison, which read, "Your 482, January 21. In the future we would suggest that you not accept reports submitted to you to be transmitted to private persons in the U.S. unless such action is advisable because of extraordinary circumstances."[24] In other words, the State Department sought to stop Harrison from collecting or sharing information about the Holocaust.

It is not hard to understand why some members of the State Department wished to stifle information about the Holocaust, given the inefficiency and willful procrastination evident among State officials with regard to the Rumanian rescue proposal. Since the flow of information would provide ammunition to State Department critics in the Treasury, a department official, probably Breckinridge Long, decided to stop the information at

22 Wyman, *The Abandonment*, 51.
23 Blum, 209.
24 Paraphrase of telegram sent from American Legation, Bern to under secretary of state, Washington, DC, 21 January 1943. Online by PBS, *America and the Holocaust*. www.pbs.org

its source.[25] Nevertheless, State's decision to cut the cables did not remain a secret forever.

Unfortunately for the State Department, Treasury officials eventually found a reference to State's deceitful cable in another message from Harrison. Thinking that the original cable might contain more information on the Riegner plan, Secretary of the Treasury Morgenthau requested a copy from the State Department. State complied, but Long removed the reference to cable 482—the one with the Riegner report—making it appear as though the State Department was not referring to the blocking of information on the Holocaust. Unbeknownst to State, Treasury official Josiah DuBois had already seen the original cable, realized what was missing, and obtained a true copy for his boss, Henry Morgenthau.[26] Now an infuriated Morgenthau and his colleagues had proof of the State Department's determination to suppress information on one of the greatest crimes against humanity.

Although he was only thirty years old, DuBois already had experience dealing with the Roosevelt administration's indifference toward Jews. On a trip to Algiers with the Foreign Funds Control in early 1943, he learned that over 4,000 Jews were interned near the Morocco-Algeria border. Though the American Jewish Joint Distribution Committee provided money for their release after the Allies took over the region, the Jews were not immediately set free. DuBois confronted the US consul about the release of the Jews, which occurred a few months later.[27] Though DuBois' contribution to the Jews' release remains unclear, the experience left little doubt in his mind that the US government had a lackadaisical attitude toward aiding Jews. When he struggled to get a copy of the State Department's original cable to Harrison, he became suspicious. As he pressured State, some officials tried to force him to drop the issue.[28] Fortunately, their comments

---

25   Feingold, 178.
26   Medoff, *Blowing the Whistle*, 33.
27   Ibid., 14.
28   Ibid., 22.

convinced DuBois to work harder until he gained access to the original cable.

The information collected by the Treasury was not enough by itself to wrest control of the refugee problem from the State Department. Action had to be taken by the men of the Treasury Department and ultimately by FDR for change to occur. A draft of an executive order was presented to Morgenthau to take to the president. The order called for a refugee committee independent of the State Department.[29] Still Morgenthau hesitated to confront FDR directly with State's treachery.

The Foreign Funds Control staff, led by Josiah DuBois, wrote a report for Morgenthau attempting to convince him that it was futile to continue to deal with State. DuBois felt so strongly about State's duplicity that he worked on Christmas Day to complete the report. Its title, "The Acquiescence of this Government in the Murder of the Jews," made it clear that the State Department was unqualified to deal with refugee matters. DuBois wrote, "I am convinced ... that certain officials in our State Department ... have been guilty not only of gross procrastination and willful failure to act, but even of willful attempts to prevent action from being taken to rescue Jews from Hitler."[30] DuBois cited the lack of State Department support for the Riegner plan as well as visa restrictions which admitted fewer refugees than were allowed under the quota. Then DuBois mentioned an issue that especially incensed Morgenthau—the suppression of information about the Holocaust. As DuBois pointed out, State concealed information not only from the public, but also from other government officials such as Morgenthau by not sharing the full content of their cables.[31] After he completed his report, DuBois could only hope that Morgenthau would use his relationship with FDR to wrest control of refugee matters away from State. Failing that, DuBois

---

29   Ibid., 33–4.
30   Ibid., 40.
31   Ibid., 50.

decided that he would resign and take the report to the press.[32]

Luckily for DuBois' career, Morgenthau's frustration with Secretary Hull and the rest of the State Department had reached boiling point. When Morgenthau spoke with Hull to discuss the cutting of the cables, Hull, though shocked, appeared "harassed and weary," "not well informed as to what was going on," and "simply bewildered."[33] Now Morgenthau was convinced that Hull would not remove Breckinridge Long or any of the people responsible for suppressing information on the Holocaust and interfering with rescue efforts. His disgust made Morgenthau receptive to the idea of appointing a special committee for refugees. After reading DuBois' report, he requested that another version be written for the president. John Pehle wrote "The Personal Report to the President," which Morgenthau would present to President Roosevelt.[34] It contained less inflammatory language but retained all the facts from the original document. It also emphasized the need for quick action. In an interview years later, John Pehle explained that State's suppression of information and its attempts to cover up its actions "were the final straws in causing the Secretary to go ahead with the President on the establishment of the War Refugee Board."[35]

Morgenthau's decision to speak with the president about the so-called Jewish Problem was not reached lightly. Morgenthau's daughter realized what her father risked by bringing up such an explosive topic with FDR. She said, "I think it must have been difficult for him to push the issue to the extent that he did when he felt that he just had to go circumvent the State Department at any cost. I think he felt he was pushing the boundaries of his relationship [with FDR]. But I think he felt by that time so strongly that something had to be done that he was willing to

---

32 Ibid., 53.

33 Blum, 220.

34 Medoff, *Blowing the Whistle*, 53.

35 John Pehle on Establishing the War Refugee Board, interview transcript online by PBS, *America and the Holocaust*. www.pbs.org

take that chance."[36] While Morgenthau risked a friendship, the younger members of the Treasury Department, none of whom were Jewish, risked their livelihoods and reputations to fight for Jews in distant lands. After all, Roosevelt had appointed the men in the State Department, including Breckinridge Long, to their present positions and might take offense at the suggestion that he had chosen poorly.

At Morgenthau's request, FDR agreed to meet with members of the Treasury at the White House on January 17, 1944.[37] The men who had uncovered State's deliberate failure to act hoped that their boss could persuade the president to act on behalf of the surviving Jews in Europe.

36   Joan Morgenthau on Her Father's Frustration with the State Department, interview transcript online by PBS, *America and the Holocaust*. www.pbs.org

37   Medoff, *Blowing the Whistle*, 54.

CHAPTER THREE

FDR's Belated Plan of Action: The Creation of the War Refugee Board, January 1944

ON THE AFTERNOON OF JANUARY 16, 1944, Secretary of the Treasury Henry Morgenthau and two other Treasury Department officials, Randolph Paul and John Pehle, met with President Roosevelt in the Oval Office for an unusual conference.[1] The meeting was unusual in part because that date was a Sunday—a day on which the president almost never conducted official business. It was also unusual because although the conference lasted only twenty minutes, the result was the creation of a new government agency.

The Treasury officials presented to FDR a report with the innocuous title: "Personal Report to the President." However, this seemingly harmless document contained information damaging to the reputation of the US government. Although John Pehle, future director of the War Refugee Board, had toned down some of the language of the original draft, the report was still a scathing indictment of the State Department. It said State Department officials "not only failed to use the governmental machinery at their disposal to rescue Jews from Hitler, but have gone so far as to use this governmental machinery to prevent the rescue of these Jews."[2] The report also pointed out that instead of trying to gather more

---

1 John Pehle, memorandum for the secretary's files, 16 January 1944; in Henry Morgenthau, *Diaries of Henry Morgenthau, Jr.* (Book 694), 190.

2 Josiah E. DuBois, Jr., interview by Lawrence Jarvik, Camden, NJ, 23 October 1978; quoted in Rafael Medoff, *Blowing the Whistle on Genocide* (West Lafayette, IN: Purdue University Press, 2009), 54.

information on the Holocaust, members of the State Department attempted to "stop the obtaining of information concerning the murder of the Jewish people of Europe."[3] As noted in Chapter Two, State blocked cables about Nazi atrocities that reliable informants tried to send to the US.

Nevertheless, the report did not lay all the blame for the fate of the Jews on the State Department. Instead, it stated that "there is a growing number of people and organizations today who have ceased to view our failure as the product of simple incompetence on the part of those officials in the State Department charged with handling this problem. They see plain anti-Semitism motivating the actions of these State Department officials, and, rightly or wrongly, it will require little more in the way of proof for this suspicion to explode into a nasty scandal."[4] Public opinion on the rescue of Jews must have changed dramatically for the Treasury Department to imply that no one, not even the president himself, would be immune from blame if the contents of the report were widely known.

Up until this meeting FDR showed little interest in the fate of Europe's Jews, just as he showed little interest in the plight of African American workers until black leaders announced their intention to march on Washington. His indifference to the Jews was not, as some historians have claimed, the result of a lack of knowledge. While major newspapers frequently buried short news reports of Hitler's crimes on the sixth or seventh page, FDR had inside information on what was really happening. The president had read the Riegner report, which contained information on the Nazi plan to exterminate the Jews. He had also spent over an hour with Jan Karski, a Polish underground leader, who witnessed the gassing of Jews in a concentration camp. Karski told Roosevelt, "I am convinced that there is no exaggeration in the accounts of the plight of the Jews. Our underground authorities are absolutely sure

---

3   Ibid.

4   John Pehle and Josiah DuBois, *Personal Report to the President*; quoted in Arthur Morse, *While Six Million Died: A Chronicle of American Apathy* (Woodstock, NY: The Overlook Press, 1983), 79.

that the Germans are out to exterminate the entire population of Europe."[5] The president liked to use the excuse that winning World War II was the best way to save Europe's Jews. Yet as the war dragged on, millions of Jews were slaughtered, making it less likely that great numbers would be alive at the war's end. Still the president failed to act on any rescue proposals brought to his attention until that Sunday afternoon in 1944. Why did the president of the United States ignore this humanitarian crisis?

FDR was above all a brilliant politician, but this strength proved to be a liability for Jews attempting to immigrate to the US, as they had no political clout that would make the president sensitive to their issues. It is true that there were plenty of American Jews with voting power, but they identified so strongly with the social-justice concept of the New Deal that Jewish political leaders who advocated for more attention to Jewish rescue could not threaten that Jews would withdraw their votes. The few businesses in America that were hiring did not want Jews, but the New Deal relief programs did not discriminate against them. Thus in the 1940 presidential election, FDR won 90 percent of the Jewish vote despite the fact that he made no commitments to help Jewish refugees.[6] America's Jews literally could not afford to lose the jobs FDR's programs provided.

Another reason American Jews supported Roosevelt was the inclusion of Jews in his administration. Yet as historian Rafael Medoff points out, few Jews in the administration held positions of authority. Those who did tended not to challenge FDR's position on immigration.[7] Only one member of FDR's cabinet, Secretary of the Treasury Henry Morgenthau, was Jewish, and even he was reluctant to ask FDR to act on the Jewish Problem until late in the

5   Jan Ciechanowski, *Defeat in Victory* (Garden City, NY: Doubleday, 1947), 182; quoted in Doris Kearns Goodwin, *No Ordinary Time* (New York: Simon & Schuster, Inc., 1994), 454.

6   *America and the Holocaust: Deceit and Indifference*, prod. Marty Ostrow, 60 min., PBS, 1993, videocassette.

7   Rafael Medoff, *FDR and the Holocaust: A Breach of Faith* (Washington, DC: The David Wyman Institute for Holocaust Studies, 2013), 14.

war. The FDR administration employed Jews but only those who were unlikely to press the president on immigration.

FDR also did not want any confrontation with restrictionists in Congress, who were opposed to increasing the immigration quotas. For example, in 1939 he needed the help of Southern Democrats to revise the Neutrality Act, which prevented the British from receiving American supplies during the war. Since they opposed changing the immigration laws, he decided that he could not allow his supposed sympathy for the Jews to get in the way of this critical task.[8] Although FDR signed the Neutrality Act in the first place, he admitted that he regretted signing it.[9] The Jews of Europe must have also regretted the president's mistake, since they experienced even more perilous conditions than the British population.

FDR's personal opinion of European immigrants also inhibited a compassionate response to the Holocaust, just as his opinion of Japanese Americans led to their internment in 1942. For example, in his April 23, 1925 column for the *Macon Daily Telegraph*, FDR wrote that immigration to the US should be restricted and limited to those who had "blood of the right sort."[10] Even then, immigrants must be distributed throughout the country so there would not be too many of them in any one area. Since FDR wanted to limit immigration, he was happy not only to uphold the strict immigration quotas he had inherited from previous administrations, but also to leave quota slots unfilled. More than 190,000 additional immigrants from Germany and other Axis countries could have entered the US between 1933 and 1945, without the quotas being exceeded.[11] FDR's desire to limit the number of Jews in the US prevented him from meeting even the

---

8   Robert N. Rosen, *Saving the Jews: Franklin D. Roosevelt and the Holocaust* (New York: Thunder's Mouth Press, 2006), 86.

9   George Brown Tindall and David E. Shi, *America: A Narrative History*, 4th ed., vol.2 (New York: W. W. Norton and Co., 1997), 894.

10   Medoff, *FDR and the Holocaust*, 26.

11   Ibid., 2.

already strict immigration quotas.

A few members of Congress who disagreed with the president and their nativist colleagues drafted the Wagner-Rogers Bill. If passed, the bill would allow 20,000 Jewish children to enter the US outside the quota. Despite the fact that the children were supposed to return to Europe after the war, congressional and public opposition to the bill was immediate. Even the president's cousin, Laura Delano, commented that "twenty thousand charming children would all too soon grow into 20,000 ugly adults."[12] As adults, they would compete for American jobs—an idea that was anathema to the American public and its congressional representatives. When the bill crossed his desk, FDR wrote "no action" on it and the plan to save Jewish children died in committee.[13]

Both the American public and the United States government reacted much differently to British children who lived in the war zone. The State Department initially raised objections, claiming that if a German torpedo struck a ship carrying British children to the United States, America would become embroiled in the war. Nevertheless, public opinion favored bringing British children to safety in the United States. In late June 1940, a Gallup poll showed 58 percent of Americans thought British children should come to America for the duration of the war.[14] Meanwhile, Congressman Thomas Hennings introduced a bill that permitted unarmed US ships to evacuate refugee children. The bill passed and British children came to America.[15] Perhaps government officials eased their consciences with the Hennings Bill, as it proved the United States was committed to bringing imperiled children from overseas to America. It did not, however, offer Europe's most endangered youngsters—Jewish children—a safe haven in the land of liberty.

Though unused quota slots existed, the US Department of

---

12   Ostrow, *America and the Holocaust.*
13   Ibid.
14   Feingold, 151.
15   Ibid., 153.

the Interior offered the president a unique way of circumventing immigration laws altogether. The department's members drafted a proclamation suggesting that the US Virgin Islands be used as a haven for Jewish refugees. The proclamation proposed to admit the refugees as temporary visitors who would therefore not be subject to immigration quotas or screening by American consuls.[16] Once again, FDR decided not to bypass the immigration laws and potentially antagonize nativist congressmen. Assistant Secretary of State Breckinridge Long wrote in his diary, "I called the President again and told him the situation. He was still more provoked and said that he would send an order over there [to the Department of the Interior] suspending the proclamation and authorized me to proceed with the scheme along the lines of his policy."[17] In fact FDR was much more concerned about his own future in politics if he were to stand up to Congress. He did nothing to jeopardize his popularity, even if taking a stand on Jewish rescue would save lives.

FDR's appointment of his friend Breckinridge Long as Assistant Secretary of State in January of 1940 ensured that few Jews would enter the US.[18] As the chief government official in charge of refugee matters, Long had the power to create new immigration restrictions, and he had no intention of relaxing the strict immigration laws. In his diary entry for October 3, 1940, Long recorded that "when I saw him [FDR] this morning the whole subject of immigration, visas, safety of the United States, procedures to be followed; and all that sort of thing was on the table ... I left him with the satisfactory thought that he was wholeheartedly in support of the policy which would resolve in favor of the United States any doubts about the admissibility of any individual."[19] Unfortunately

16   Breckinridge Long, *The War Diary of Breckinridge Long: Selections from the Years 1939–1944*, comp. and ed. Fred L. Israel (Lincoln, NE: University of Nebraska Press, 1966), 152.
17   Ibid.
18   Fred L. Israel, introduction to *The War Diary of Breckinridge Long*, by Breckinridge Long, xxiv.
19   Long, 134–5.

for Jews trying to leave Europe for the United States, Long was correct. Along with his concern that refugees might become public charges, FDR worried that Nazi agents were infiltrating the US disguised as refugees. Ironically FDR's only close encounter with espionage was via an anti-Semitic clerk in the US Embassy in London, who stole secret correspondence between FDR and Churchill. The documents were passed to the Nazi Foreign Office and the Germans discovered some US codes.[20] Nevertheless, the incident rattled FDR. Afterward, whenever the president was requested by a compassionate group or a government official to loosen his policy on immigration, the nativist Long only needed to bring up the possibility of Jews entering as Nazi agents, and FDR would turn down the request. Unsurprisingly, Long noted in 1941 that the president agreed with his proposal to scrutinize potential immigrants who had close relatives in Germany and Russia.[21]

FDR also made it clear that he wanted Long to have the greatest influence on refugee policy. When the Justice Department questioned whether they or the State Department should control immigration and refugee matters, FDR answered, "I want control in the Department of State."[22] For the most part FDR left State Department officials in charge of refugee and immigration issues. He did not ask questions about the department's activities because he knew his desire to limit immigration would be acted upon by Long.

Yet when Treasury Department members presented FDR with their report, John Pehle recorded that "the President listened attentively and seemed to grasp the significance of the various points."[23] Although he had insisted for years that nothing could be done for the Jews outside of winning the war, on that Sunday afternoon FDR agreed with Henry Morgenthau's assertion that "effective action could be taken" to rescue the Jews, particularly those

---

20   Rosen, 194.
21   Long, 213.
22   Ibid., 222.
23   Pehle, memorandum for the secretary's files, *Diaries of Henry Morgenthau*, 190.

from Rumania and France.[24] FDR's sudden interest in Europe's Jews was not, as some historians have argued, evidence of his humanitarianism.[25] Ever the politician, FDR knew the threat of a public scandal in early 1944 was very real. Even before the general public became aware of the report's contents, an outcry had already broken out over Assistant Secretary of State Breckinridge Long's testimony at the House Foreign Affairs Committee hearings.

Prior to the hearings, the House of Representatives was considering a resolution to call for the establishment of a separate agency outside of the State Department for refugees. After a group of rabbis unsuccessfully approached the president with petitions for a rescue agency, Peter Bergson, the master of public relations, leapt into action. The Bergson group convinced some powerful members of Congress to consider creating a new rescue agency. Will Rogers, Jr., one of the congressmen who Bergson persuaded, could not understand why FDR had not acted on behalf of Europe's Jews. Rogers desperately wanted "the United States—as a country and as a nation—to protest and stand for the rescue of these people when it could be done."[26] Thanks to the efforts of congressmen like Rogers and other Bergson supporters, in November of 1943 the House drafted a resolution that stated, "the House of Representatives recommends and urges the creation by the President of a committee of diplomatic, economic, and military experts to formulate and effectuate a plan of immediate action designed to save the surviving Jewish people of Europe from extinction at the hands of Nazi Germany."[27] Still, not all members of the House Foreign Affairs Committee could agree on the resolution, so private hearings were held, during which witnesses testified for and against.

Not surprisingly Assistant Secretary of State Long testified against the resolution. He told the committee that such an agency

---

24   Ibid.

25   Yehuda Bauer, *A History of the Holocaust* (Danbury, CT: Franklin Watts, 1982), 317.

26   Will Rogers, Jr., interview by Marty Ostrow, 1993, *America and the Holocaust.*

27   *Problems of World War II and its Aftermath, Part 2, Selected Executive Session Hearings of the Committee, 1943–50* (Washington, DC: US House of Representatives, 1976), 15–16.

was unnecessary because "We have taken into this country, since the beginning of the Hitler regime and the persecution of the Jews, until today, approximately 580,000 refugees."[28] Committee members who desired to look favorably upon their government's intentions toward Jewish refugees, as well as those who did not want the resolution passed, believed Long's story. Then L ong made the mistake of allowing his testimony to be published. Though m any U S n ewspapers r epeated h is s tatements w ithout questioning them, a few news outlets and Jewish organizations pointed out the inconsistencies in Long's statement. The usually unobtrusive Commission on Rescue of the American Jewish Conference asked the overlooked question: "To whom were those visas issued? Mr. Long's testimony tended to create the erroneous impression that all 580,000 were Jews."[29] According to the Immigration and Naturalization Service, however, the number of Jews who came in under national quotas between January 1, 1933 and June 30, 1943 totaled 166,843.[30] Long later claimed that he should have said that 568,000 visas were authorized of which 545,000 were issued.[31] His retraction statement still failed to explain why he had implied that most of those refugees were Jews when he had done everything in his power to prevent Jews from entering the US since his appointment as assistant secretary of state.

The press made Long a laughingstock, much to the chagrin of the congressmen who wished to believe that Long had genuine concern for refugees. The public humiliation of Long made the members of Congress who had introduced the resolution more determined than ever to support a separate rescue commission

---

28   Adolph Held, Chairman of Jewish Labor Committee to Assistant Secretary of State Breckinridge Long, 17 December 1943, Papers of the War Refugee Board, ed. Robert Lester, (Bethesda, MD: UPA collection from LexisNexis, 2002–6).

29   Statement by the Commission on Rescue of the American Jewish Conference, 27 December 1943, Papers of the War Refugee Board.

30   Ibid.

31   Long, 334–5.

for refugees. The idea of creating a separate agency for refugees gained support in both the House and Senate. On January 24, 1944 Congress planned to put the resolution to a vote in the Senate, and polls showed that it almost certainly would pass.[32]

The report from the Treasury Department could not have been presented to the president at a more auspicious time. While Congress could only suggest that the president create a new rescue agency, the politically astute FDR would not want Congress to take credit for the idea. Furthermore, any scandal associated with his administration during an election year like 1944 would be disastrous. Long was now a political liability rather than an asset who enabled the president to ignore refugee issues. Pehle noted during the meeting that the president, who had appointed Long, was reluctant to believe that his friend had deliberately obstructed opportunities to rescue Jews.[33] Following FDR's conference with the Treasury Department officials, Long continued to serve as Assistant Secretary of State; however, his duties were curtailed and he was passed over for political appointments in favor of less experienced men.[34]

Secretary of the Treasury Henry Morgenthau and John Pehle brought a draft of an executive order to create the War Refugee Board to the meeting. Under this plan, Long's authority over refugee matters would be revoked. When the three Treasury Department officials finished making their case for a new refugee rescue agency, they presented the executive order to the president. He suggested that the secretary of war be added to the Board in addition to the secretary of state and secretary of the treasury.[35] At the end of the meeting, FDR made the promise the Treasury Department attendees had hoped to hear when he said, "We will do it."[36]

32   David S. Wyman, *The Abandonment of the Jews* (New York: The New Press, 1984), 204.

33   Pehle, memorandum for the secretary's files, *Diaries of Henry Morgenthau*, 191.

34   Long, 366.

35   Pehle, memorandum for the secretary's files, *Diaries of Henry Morgenthau*, 190.

36   Martin Ostrow, Interview with John Pehle, Bethesda, MD, 2 October 1991, quoted in Rafael Medoff, *Blowing the Whistle on Genocide*, 64.

After the meeting, FDR sent a memo to Secretary of State Cordell Hull. He wrote, "I have been deeply concerned for a long time with the cowardly persecution of the Jews by the Nazis ... In view of the growing criticism of our efforts to date, I think it is also important that we let our own people know of our determination to do all that is within our power to save these people."[37] Later in the memo FDR stated that he attached a letter containing the proposal for the War Refugee Board, which he wanted the State Department to approve. Fortunately Undersecretary of State Edward Stettinius approved of the draft executive order. He told members of the Treasury, "I think it is wonderful."[38] His endorsement alleviated any doubts FDR may have held that the WRB was a viable solution to his public relations problem.

As noted above, FDR's concern for the Jews was a recent development, which happened to coincide with congressional pressure and the threat of a political scandal. Despite his friendship with the president, Secretary of the Treasury Morgenthau confirmed this at a March 1944 Treasury Department meeting. He stated that "the thing that made it possible to get the President to really act ... was ... that the resolution at least had passed the Senate to form this kind of a War Refugee Committee."[39] Only the growing criticism from others and Treasury's discovery of the State Department's questionable actions motivated the president to aid the Jews at the end of the war. The executive order establishing the War Refugee Board was signed by FDR on January 22, 1944, just six days after his meeting with the three Treasury Department officials and two days before the Senate was scheduled to vote on its resolution.[40] Historian Yehuda Bauer agreed that FDR's decision to form the WRB in early 1944 was at least partly motivated by changes in

---

37 Franklin D. Roosevelt, memorandum to the secretary of state, January 1944, Papers of the War Refugee Board.
38 Pehle, memorandum for the Secretary's Files, *Diaries of Henry Morgenthau*, 192.
39 *Diaries of Henry Morgenthau*. (Book 707), 220.
40 Franklin D. Roosevelt, Executive Order No. 9417, 22 January 1944, Papers of the War Refugee Board.

Congress and in American public opinion. He stated, "The climate of public opinion was changing in America. Attacks in the press and in Congress on government inaction in matters of rescue, especially of Jews, were multiplying ... Anti-Semitic sentiment was declining."[41] Motivated by political and public pressure as well as the possibility of a scandal in his administration, FDR signed the executive order that created the WRB.

Executive Order 9417 not only created the War Refugee Board but also endowed it with unprecedented authority. The order stated that "the functions of the Board shall include *without limitation* [my italics] the development of plans and programs and the inauguration of effective measures for (a) the rescue, transportation, maintenance and relief of the victims of enemy oppression, and (b) the establishment of havens of temporary refuge for such victims."[42] Whereas before the US government had shown no interest in the fate of Europe's Jews, the WRB now had carte blanche from the president to save lives. In the past, resistance from the State Department was a major roadblock to Jewish rescue; however, the president's order commanded the State, Treasury and War Departments to cooperate with the Board and support its rescue plans via information and supplies.[43] The president also pledged his support for the WRB's activities. The new agency was instructed to report to FDR "at frequent intervals."[44]

In keeping with FDR's wishes, the State Department wasted no time in promoting the new rescue policy. The secretary of state sent a telegram to US consuls January 25, telling them to do everything to stop the persecution of Jews in their assigned countries.[45] They were

---

41   Yehuda Bauer, *A History of the Holocaust*, 317.

42   Franklin D. Roosevelt, Executive Order No. 9417, 22 January 1944, Papers of the War Refugee Board..

43   Ibid.

44   Ibid.

45   Cordell Hull, telegram sent to American Embassy, London No. 634, midnight, 25 January 1944, Papers of the War Refugee Board.

requested to report on what was already being done to help Jews, make suggestions for future rescue and relief, and to approach the leaders of countries in which they were accredited to determine whether the governments were willing to help out.[46] American consuls abroad had previously been told by the State Department to postpone the issuing of visas. Now the consuls were literally expected to change this mindset overnight and do whatever they could to facilitate rescue of and relief for Jews.

A few days later Treasury Secretary Morgenthau sent a similar telegram to US war commanders. The tone of this telegram was different from that of the State Department telegram, however. Morgenthau did not request help from members of the War Department. Instead, as the executive order entitled him to do, he told them that they must cooperate with agencies attempting to help Jews and that they were expected to suggest future rescue and relief programs.[47] Nevertheless, these demands were made with one caveat—that commanders should do everything possible to follow the executive order provided their efforts were "consistent with the successful prosecution of the war."[48]

Despite the authority granted to the WRB, its members soon realized that it would be difficult to change the attitudes of government agencies that had ignored the so-called Jewish Problem for years. In addition, though FDR signed the executive order giving power to the WRB and ordered it to report to him, he was accustomed to leaving refugee matters to others. If WRB members needed his assistance, they would have to vie for the president's attention. Henry Morgenthau realized that even with the signing of the executive order, the WRB still faced challenges. After the War Refugee Board had been established, his hopes lay in the remaining months with "crusaders, passionately persuaded of

---

46   Ibid.
47   Secretary Morgenthau to Assistant Secretary McCloy, 28 January 1944, Papers of the War Refugee Board.
48   Ibid.

the need for speed and action."[49] Fortunately for the surviving Jews in Europe, the Board's leadership and its junior members remained passionate about their mission even though the executive order did not completely remove the obstacles to successful rescue.

---

49   Henry Morgenthau on the Creation of the WRB, January 1944; quoted in John Morton Blum, *From the Morgenthau Diaries: Years of War* (Boston: Houghton Mifflin Co., 1967), 223.

CHAPTER FOUR

Theoretical V. Real Power: Limitations on the WRB's Authority

AFTER PRESIDENT ROOSEVELT ANNOUNCED THE creation of the War Refugee Board, he searched for a dynamic leader to oversee its operations. He thought someone well-known would be best suited to the post and he wasted two weeks considering various candidates without making a decision.[1] Yet those in the Treasury Department, where the WRB headquarters were housed, thought differently. They saw John Pehle as the perfect man for the job. Although only in his early thirties, Pehle had experience that would stand to help him as executive director of the Board. While FDR remained indecisive, Treasury built a compelling case for their man.

Pehle's coworkers pointed out that his work in the Treasury Foreign Funds Control Division proved that he could outsmart the Nazis by preventing them from gaining access to the financial resources of American industries.[2] He also proved his commitment to Jewish rescue by pushing for a separate agency before others did. In fact, during the January meeting with FDR, Morgenthau assigned Pehle the duty of explaining State's duplicity to the president. Pehle also had the advantage of being well liked by a variety of government officials, diplomats, and organizations. For example, Pehle's commitment to Jewish rescue won him the support of Jewish

---

1   Wyman, *The Abandonment*, 211.
2   Letter from Randolph Paul to Bruce Bliven, 4 February 1944, Papers of the War Refugee Board.

organizations like the World Jewish Congress, the American Jewish Joint Distribution Committee (JDC), and the Emergency Committee to Save the Jewish People of Europe.[3] Though these organizations did not always agree, they agreed that Pehle should run the WRB. As for FDR's concern that he needed a "man with a name," Treasury members pointed out that well-known people had worked on the refugee issue for years without success.[4] By early February 1944 FDR sided with the Treasury Department and appointed Pehle Executive Director of the War Refugee Board.[5] The duties of the executive director included implementing the Board's rescue and relief plans, but Pehle planned to go beyond the call of duty.

Pehle's most important qualification for the position was his ability to be both realistic and optimistic about his duties. As part of the team that uncovered State's treachery, he had already witnessed the indifference of many people to the fate of the Jews. Shortly after the WRB's creation, however, Pehle stated, "There has been some tendency for people to say that the task of the War Refugee Board is an impossible one, that it is too late to save more than a handfull [sic] of Jews and other persecuted minorities in Europe from Nazi extermination ... I do not share these views ... [W]hat I have seen to date convinces me that Jews and other persecuted minorities can be saved if those charged with the task think they can be saved and are determined to drive toward that end."[6] Despite the knowledge that saving Jews in Nazi-controlled territory would not be easy, Pehle was determined to save as many lives as possible. Given the limitations placed on the WRB's authority, Pehle needed to draw on that determination again and again.

---

3   DuBois, Pehle as Director of the War Refugee Board, 1 February 1944, Papers of the War Refugee Board.

4   Ibid.

5   White House Press Release, 4 February 1944, Papers of the War Refugee Board.

6   Pehle, Statement of Acting Director War Refugee Board, 4 February 1944, Papers of the War Refugee Board.

When his work was over, all Board members agreed that Pehle had done "a magnificent job" despite "tremendous hardships."[7] One of Pehle's difficulties lay in the first few lines of the executive order that created the WRB. The executive order failed to specifically mention Jews; instead, it referred to aiding "victims of enemy oppression."[8] Although he had received reliable reports of deportations, FDR was still reluctant to publicly single out Jews for US aid. Even members of the Treasury agreed that not mentioning Jews was the easiest way to get the president to sign the order.[9] Anti-Semitism was still alive and well among many American voters. Pehle encountered this prejudice the same day he was appointed as the Board's executive director. When he returned home from the office, he received a telephone call from the wife of a prominent physician. She asked if he was Jewish. When she discovered that he was not, she then asked, "Why are you doing this [serving on the Board]?"[10] It made no sense to most Americans to help Jews in Europe simply because it was the humane thing to do. Though some people used the excuse that refugees would take the few available American jobs, the doctor's wife offered no such excuse. Instead, people like her wanted to "keep America for Americans."[11] Apparently they did not see the irony in the fact that the ancestors of most American families came to the United States as immigrants.

The executive order stated that the State, Treasury, and War Departments should "supply or obtain for the Board such information and to extend to the Board such supplies, shipping and other specified assistance and facilities that the Board may require."[12]

---

7   "Why Pehle Quit War Refugee Board in Favor of O'Dwyer," *New York Post*, 29 January 1945, Papers of the War Refugee Board.

8   Executive Order 9417, Papers of the War Refugee Board.

9   Martin Ostrow, Interview with John Pehle, Bethesda, MD, 2 October 1991, quoted in Rafael Medoff, *Blowing the Whistle on Genocide*, 64.

10 Marty Ostrow, Interview with John Pehle, *America and the Holocaust*.

11 Marty Ostrow, Interview with Harry Stoeher of Patriotic Sons of America, *America and the Holocaust*.

12 Executive Order 9417, Papers of the War Refugee Board.

In reality, however, few officials outside the Treasury Department wanted to help the Jews. In spite of Secretary Hull's initial cooperation with the WRB, he happily reassigned all refugee matters to Under Secretary of State Edward Stettinius.[13] Stettinius said he approved of the Board, yet under his leadership, or lack of it, State remained a reluctant partner of the WRB. Much of the Board's contact with the State Department centered on minor officials who remained indifferent to the plight of Europe's Jews. Although the creation of the WRB removed the responsibility of rescue and relief from State, the WRB depended on State to send important cables to foreign countries and other agencies, which it did begrudgingly and sometimes not at all. Transcripts of WRB meetings frequently referred to cables "still pending" at the State Department, including one to Nazi satellite countries warning them not to participate in the extermination of the Jews.[14] State gave the bewildering explanation that such a warning would somehow induce the Nazis to kill Jews faster. With Hitler already killing tens of thousands of Jews each day, the idea that WRB propaganda would make things worse was preposterous.

State Department members made their distaste for the WRB's mission known almost as soon as the agency became functional. Soon after the WRB's creation, its members were notified of a life-or-death scenario involving over 2,000 Jews held in a concentration camp in Vittel, France. Some of these Jews obtained Latin American passports, which they thought the Nazis would accept. Instead, the Nazis insisted the passports were fake and threatened to deport the Jews. The WRB requested State's assistance in asking the neutral Swiss to intervene on behalf of the Jews, sending State drafts of cables for the Swiss in February and again in March.[15] The State Department was in no hurry to contact the Swiss or anyone else about Jews in need, even if a delay meant the loss of human lives. Henry Morgenthau bristled at State's blatant refusal to cooperate with the WRB as mandated in

13 Wyman, *The Abandonment*, 210.

14 War Refugee Board Conference, 19 February 1944, Papers of the War Refugee Board.

15 Medoff, *Blowing the Whistle*, 72.

the executive order. He said, "for a month and a half the WRB has had a cable lying over there in the State Department urging them to ask the Swiss to have the Germans recognize these people. Well two hundred and fifty of them have been moved, and that means death."[16]

Though the WRB cable finally went out in April, State Department procrastination resulted in a needless loss of lives. Once they received the cable, the Swiss exerted pressure on the Nazis. By May 11, the Nazis agreed to stop deporting Jews who had Latin American passports; however, 238 Jews from Vittel had already been killed.[17] One of the Jews deported to Auschwitz from Vittel was renowned poet Itzahak Katznelson. In his *Vittel Diary*, published after his death, he wrote, "[S]ure enough, the nations did not interfere, nor did they protest … It was as if the leaders of the nations were afraid that the killings might stop."[18] Although the staff of the WRB tried to save Katznelson and the other deported Jews, they did not have the authority that FDR or other world leaders possessed. Instead, the Board depended on the State Department to send its messages, a task for which State had no enthusiasm. The staff of the WRB deserves credit for pushing State to safeguard the lives of the remaining Jews who held Latin American passports, but such pressure should not have been necessary. The pattern of State delaying cables and WRB staff members trying to push them through continued throughout the agency's existence.

Another glaring example of State's continued hostility toward Jews occurred on March 23, 1944. The WRB prepared a message to the International Red Cross stating that the agency should demand the right to ship food and supplies to concentration camp inmates.[19] By placing more Red Cross workers in the vicinity of concentration camps, the WRB hoped to send Nazi-controlled countries the message that the world was watching and thereby get better treatment

16   Henry Morgenthau, *Diaries of Henry Morgenthau, Jr.* (Book 718), 172–3.
17   Morse, 346–7.
18   Ibid., 347.
19   For Harrison from War Refugee Board—following for Intercross, draft attached to Pehle's memo to Oscar Cox, 17 April 1944, Papers of the War Refugee Board.

for the internees. Once again the State Department left the cable in limbo for almost one month, and then insisted that London's Blockade Committee approve it.[20] State's stalling caused the usually unflappable Pehle to lose his patience. On April 17, 1944, he wrote in a memo to Treasury: "For some time the War Refugee Board has been trying to get the attached cable to the International Red Cross cleared and despatched [sic] by State … if the cable were cleared with the Blockade Committee before being transmitted to Bern, I am convinced that the delay involved in such clearance would decrease the effectiveness of the proposed action. (To put it mildly)."[21] Twelve days later, State finally sent the cable.

The State Department's lack of cooperation with the WRB extended beyond the mere delay of cables; sometimes State refused WRB requests outright. Though the executive order gave the WRB the authority to ask both the State Department and foreign countries for assistance in rescuing Jews, State remained uncooperative. In October 1944 the Emergency Committee to Save the Jewish People of Europe asked Pehle to send a cable to the governments of Poland, Italy, France, and Britain. The cable reminded these countries of their obligation to aid Jewish citizens who were being persecuted in concentration camps, particularly since they had more resources with which to aid Jews in 1944 than at the start of World War II.[22] Unfortunately the WRB, though sympathetic to the Emergency Committee's cause, did not have the authority to send the cable; it had to be approved by the State Department. With his usual promptness, Pehle sent a copy of the cable to State for approval, but State ruled that it could not send messages to foreign governments on behalf of private individuals. Instead, it suggested that the Emergency Committee send the cable on its own.[23] As State knew,

---

20   Pehle's memo to Oscar Cox, 17 April 1944, Papers of the War Refugee Board.
21   Ibid.
22   Rabbi Baruch Korff, Letter from Emergency Committee to Save the Jewish People of Europe to Pehle, 2 October 1944, Papers of the War Refugee Board.
23   John Pehle, Letter to the Emergency Committee to Save the Jewish People of Europe, 12 October 1944, Papers of the War Refugee Board.

the Emergency Committee's position would have been strengthened if the cable had the backing of the United States government. Once again, State decided not to aid European Jews.

State was not the only Department that refused to cooperate with the WRB. The War Department also showed that it had no interest in aiding Jews. Although the Secretary of War supported the idea of the Board, he was too busy trying to win the war to pay much attention to refugees. Like the Secretary of State, he handed the task of communicating with the WRB to a subordinate, Assistant Secretary John McCloy.[24] McCloy later refused to instruct the military to assist with WRB objectives. Even early on, the War Department demonstrated its indifference to WRB requests. A Board meeting transcript from February 1944 mentions the WRB's desire to have the War Department transfer one of its members, former King's County, New York District Attorney William O'Dwyer, to the Board's staff. The department denied the request, claiming that they could not spare his services.[25] Ironically, O'Dwyer eventually joined the WRB when Pehle stepped down as director.[26]

In addition to dealing with opposition from the State and War Departments, Pehle faced another obstacle: the paucity of government funds set aside for the WRB. In the *Final Summary Report* of the War Refugee Board, the amount of government funds provided to the Board was described as "very small."[27] The president allocated $1 million from his emergency fund to the WRB, which sounds like a substantial amount for any project in the 1940s. Yet this money was intended to cover all the Board's needs, including staff salaries for thirty people, expenses for government attachés abroad, supplies for refugees (food, clothes, medicine), purchase and rental of vehicles to transport refugees, and other miscellaneous

---

24 Wyman, *The Abandonment*, 210.
25 Conference Notes from WRB Meeting, 19 February 1944, Papers of the War Refugee Board.
26 "Why Pehle Quit War Refugee Board," Papers of the War Refugee Board.
27 William O'Dwyer, *Final Summary Report of the Executive Director, War Refugee Board*, 15 September 1945, Papers of the War Refugee Board.

purchases.[28] Given this list, the amount of federal funds allocated to the WRB seems almost laughable, except that human lives depended on the generosity of the United States government.

Luckily for Pehle and other members of the Board who genuinely wanted to help Jews, private Jewish and even some Christian agencies gave generously to the WRB's causes. Major contributors included the American Jewish Joint Distribution Committee, the Vaad Hatzala (an Orthodox rescue committee), and the World Jewish Congress.[29] These organizations did not need to be asked to contribute; they were just relieved that they could donate money to an agency that had the authority to help European Jews. About $20 million in private funds was donated to support the WRB's rescue and relief projects. As the *Final Summary Report* stated, no possible plan lacked funds thanks to the generosity of private agencies.[30] Without donations from private organizations, the WRB could not have helped so many victims of enemy oppression.

The president eventually allotted an additional $1,068,750 to the Board to buy and ship food parcels to concentration camps.[31] Yet the question remains—why was the government so unwilling to fund the WRB? In a memo, one of Pehle's aides insisted that the Board must be funded primarily by private agencies.[32] Unfortunately the memo does not explain why the government did not want to provide support to the WRB. According to historian David Wyman, Pehle refused to ask Congress for funds, stating in a Board staff meeting, "[T]he last thing I want you to do is go to Congress."[33] His insistence seems odd, as Congress helped create the WRB by putting pressure on FDR to create a rescue agency.

---

28 Franklin D. Roosevelt, Letter to Secretary of Treasury, 29 January 1944, Papers of the War Refugee Board.

29 William O'Dwyer, *Final Summary Report of the Executive Director, War Refugee Board*, 15 September 1945, Papers of the War Refugee Board.

30 Ibid.

31 Ibid.

32 Lawrence Lesser, War Refugee Board memo, 23 February 1944, Papers of the War Refugee Board.

33 Wyman, *The Abandonment*, 213.

Although the Senate Foreign Relations Committee passed the resolution for a new rescue agency, the entire Congress never voted on it because FDR established the Board via executive order a few days before the scheduled vote in the full Senate. Due to the multiple hearings in the House Foreign Relations Committee, the resolution never came up for a vote in the House of Representatives either. Therefore it is possible that the House Appropriations Committee members, who would have determined the WRB's budget, were not in favor of the new rescue agency. Pehle certainly believed that someone in Congress would oppose funding the WRB. Perhaps the fact that FDR created the Board just prior to the Senate's vote turned some congressmen against it. If FDR wanted all the credit for creating the WRB, and the president was rarely inclined to share credit, members of Congress may have thought that FDR should fund the agency himself.

FDR and other government officials also may have discovered what Pehle already learned from the phone call he received after taking his WRB post—plenty of American voters did not care what happened to the Jews of Europe. By design, Jews were never specifically mentioned in the executive order, though the WRB's activities revolved around aid for Jewish refugees. FDR quickly lost interest in the WRB after its creation. He occasionally made a speech on its behalf, but he almost always needed to be persuaded by WRB members, who would then write a statement for him. Even Jewish members of Congress rarely brought up the issue of Jewish refugees.

The reluctance of Congress and the president to support the new rescue agency stemmed from the public's dislike of Jews. According to public opinion polls taken during World War II, about one-third of the American public was anti-Semitic.[34] Various reasons existed for the highest level of anti-Semitism ever documented in the United States. For example, some Americans blamed the Jews for the Depression of the previous decade.[35] They thought Jews had too

---

34 Wyman, *A Race Against Death*, 3.
35 Ibid.

much economic and political power, though in reality Jews struggled to find jobs during the Depression and were often discriminated against simply because of their ethnicity. Some religious leaders sought to capitalize on American anti-Semitism and effectively promoted their messages of hatred. The most influential leader was Father Charles E. Coughlin, an anti-Semitic priest whose radio broadcasts reached millions of listeners every Sunday.[36] Some non-Jewish leaders opposed Coughlin's messages, but many more chose to remain silent. Many ordinary Americans also saw no reason to help a religious and ethnic minority in a part of the world they had never visited. If voters showed little interest, elected officials had no motivation to support the WRB.

Though the generosity of charitable organizations provided much-needed funds for WRB projects, the lack of government funds remained problematic. The failure of the Roosevelt administration to fund the WRB showed the world that the United States government was not committed to Jewish rescue. Without government funding and support the WRB became a facilitator of projects recommended by charitable organizations, not the powerful government agency that the executive order had promised.

Ultimately the greatest difficulty that Pehle and his staff encountered was poor timing. FDR created the War Refugee Board on January 22, 1944, nearly three years after the United States had entered World War II. It came too late for the 4 million Jews whom the Nazis had already murdered during the period of Allied apathy. Though he took his post willingly, Pehle recognized that there were limits to what the Board could accomplish so late in the war.[37] DuBois, the man whose memo on the State Department's obstruction of information caused Morgenthau to confront FDR, also complained that once the WRB was established, "it was too damned late to do much."[38] Nevertheless, WRB members never succumbed to Peter Bergson's sense of

---

36   Ibid.

37   Marty Ostrow, Interview with John Pehle, *America and the Holocaust.*

38   Wyman, *The Abandonment*, 287.

failure after the creation of the Board.[39] In contrast, Pehle, DuBois, and the other members of the WRB staff committed themselves to aiding the Jews who were still alive in Europe.

---

39   Peter Bergson, Interview with David Wyman, 13–15 April 1973, *A Race Against Death*, 160.

CHAPTER FIVE

Negotiating with the Enemy: The WRB's Response to Rescue Offers for Jews

ALTHOUGH 4 MILLION JEWS HAD already been murdered by the time the War Refugee Board was created, opportunities existed in 1944 to save the surviving Jews, especially in Hungary. As the ink dried on the executive order that established the WRB, 800,000 Jews still lived in Hungary.[1] Their safety was by no means assured, however. To borrow a phrase from the executive order itself, they were in imminent danger of death. Deportations of 437,000 Jews occurred after the German occupation in March.[2] The fate of Hungary's Jews seemed bleak, but the United States and its allies received several proposals from Hungarian and Nazi officials that involved exchanges of Allied goods in return for Jewish emigration from Nazi territories. Occasionally, Jewish refugees were offered to the Allies without any demand for goods. The War Refugee Board participated in negotiations for Jewish rescue throughout 1944. But the WRB's efforts were often hampered by a variety of limitations placed upon it by other nations, the United States government, and even its own members.

On July 6, 1944 Hungarian regent Miklós Horthy, who had previously cooperated with the Nazis, had a sudden change of heart. First, he ordered a halt to Jewish deportations. He then made a strange offer to the American and British governments. Horthy agreed to release

---

1   Yehuda Bauer, *Rethinking the Holocaust* (New Haven, CT: 2001), 224.
2   Ibid., 226.

certain Jews if he had the assurances of their resettlement in Allied or neutral countries. For example, Jews who had connections in Sweden or were of Swedish nationality could immigrate there. The British authorities authorized immigration of several thousand Jews to Palestine.[3] At the urging of the War Refugee Board, Horthy also agreed to send Jewish children under age ten to Palestine. The offer included a total of 17,000–20,000 young people.[4] Horthy's proposal differed markedly from other rescue proposals in that he never requested money or goods in exchange for releasing the Jews.

What motivated the Hungarian regent to release Jews without material gain? Sympathy for the Jewish people was not prevalent in Hungary. By the summer of 1944, however, Western democracies were putting pressure on the people of Hungary, warning them of repercussions if they complied with the Nazis' plan to exterminate Jews. An editorial in the British paper *The Manchester Guardian* stated, "[I]t was not until Mr. Eden and Mr. Roosevelt had promised reprisals for the guilty and until the King of Sweden, the Pope and neutral governments had made appeals to him that the Regent attempted to intervene."[5] Still, rescue advocates, including the staff at the War Refugee Board, thought the offer should be explored regardless of Horthy's motives. The WRB sent Henry Morgenthau and Josiah DuBois to London to work on a joint American and British response to the offer. It soon became apparent that the British did not share the WRB's enthusiasm for rescuing Jews, particularly since Horthy's offer involved the immigration of more Jews to Palestine. As *The Manchester Guardian* pointed out, 30,000 Jews remained in Hungary and about 14,000 permits existed for Palestine in 1944.[6] Throughout the war, the British resisted Jewish immigration to Palestine and they responded similarly to the

---

3   *The Present State of Measures Taken by the Hungarian Government with Regard to the Jews*, Budapest, 18 July 1944, Papers of the War Refugee Board.

4   Feingold, 267.

5   Telegram from George Winant, American ambassador to Britain to US secretary of state, 5 August 1944, Papers of the War Refugee Board.

6   Ibid.

Hungarian government's proposal.

While in London DuBois sent a copy to the War Refugee Board of the joint British and American response to Horthy's offer. It did not offer Jews sanctuary in Palestine. Instead, "despite the heavy difficulties and responsibilities involved," the two governments offered to care for Jews "leaving Hungary who reach neutral or United Nations territory."[7] Interestingly the neutral countries involved had yet to be notified of their role in saving Hungarian Jews as decided by Britain and America. As it turned out, the neutrals did not object to receiving Jews from Hungary, and John Pehle was finally able to respond to the Horthy offer a month later. Sadly the drawn-out negotiations between the British and American governments made the neutrals' cooperation irrelevant. By August 17 Pehle noted that the Germans objected to the emigration of Jews from Hungary unless the Germans received some sort of ransom.[8] Both Pehle and the State Department opposed entering into any ransom negotiations with the Nazis. If America and Britain had formed a joint resolution sooner, however, thousands of Hungarian Jews might have escaped. The two democracies instead gave the Germans plenty of time to object to Horthy's plan.

Britain hurt Allied opportunities to rescue Hungarian Jews by refusing to accept additional refugees to Palestine, but the United States was not blameless either. In part the WRB had difficulty convincing the British to accept Horthy's offer because of America's past lack of interest in and at times hostility toward Jewish rescue. The United States had shown no signs of wishing to rescue European Jews until the creation of the WRB in 1944. Even then, the executive order that created the Board failed to specifically identify Jews as the main candidates for rescue and relief.[9] The history of American inaction on Jewish immigration and rescue led the British to believe

---

7   Telegram for the WRB from DuBois, 16 August 1944, Papers of the War Refugee Board.

8   Memo from Mr. Pehle to Mr. Stettinius, 17 August 1944, Papers of the War Refugee Board.

9   Executive Order 9417, Papers of the War Refugee Board.

that the WRB was a symbolic gesture to American Jews rather than a working agency.[10] British doubt of the sincerity of America's commitment to Europe's Jews contributed to the inability of the WRB to act on the Horthy offer. If the British had known of the struggles of men like DuBois and Pehle to get the WRB created and their genuine desire to help whomever they could, more Hungarian Jews might have survived the war.

In addition to offers from Nazi satellite countries like Hungary, individual Nazis demonstrated their willingness to negotiate for Jewish lives. Joel Brand, a Hungarian native and a member of the Vaadat Ezra Vehatzala (Assistance and Rescue Committee), left for Istanbul, Turkey in May to discuss a proposal with Nazi officials. Nazi leader Adolf Eichmann told Brand what the Nazis wanted as ransom for the Jews. In exchange for 10,000 trucks (which they promised not to use on the Western Front), 2 million bars of soap, 800 tons of coffee, 200 tons of cocoa and 800 tons of tea, "the Germans would liberate all the Jews in Nazi-occupied countries [not just Hungarian Jews] and permit them to travel to neutral areas."[11] If Brand returned to Istanbul with Allied acceptance of the proposal, the Nazis promised to release the first transport of Jews before receiving any goods.

Brand served only as a Jewish relief worker in Hungary, with connections in neutral countries; he was not an agent of the WRB or the United States government. Lack of familiarity with Brand and distrust of the Nazis combined with the Allies' usual inertia on Jewish rescue led to objections to the Brand proposal. One legitimate concern was that the Nazis were using the Brand proposal to seek a separate peace with the West while breaking up the alliance with the Soviets.[12] After all, the Nazis promised not to use any trucks they acquired from the deal on the Western Front. They said

10   Feingold, 268.
11   Report prepared by Reuben B. Resnik at request of Ambassador Steinhardt in Care of American Consulate General, Istanbul, 4 June 1944, Papers of the War Refugee Board.
12   Ibid.

nothing about the Eastern Front. The idea of Nazis benefiting from their mistreatment of the Jews was reprehensible, but so were some Allied objections. For example, the argument that letting Jews go would make the Nazis look more humanitarian had a few holes in it. In the first place, what difference did it make if the proposal improved the image of the Nazis as long as it saved lives? Secondly, the extermination of millions of Jews had already occurred and the Nazis were capable of killing even more. Another interpretation of the proposal was that the Germans were refusing to provide subsistence for Jews in Nazi-controlled territories by dumping them on the Allies.[13] Once again America and Britain showed a reluctance to help even those Jews who were in imminent danger of death.

By June 4 the American Jewish Joint Distribution Committee representative in Istanbul sent a report to Washington which stated that the proposal could not be carried out. The report did not recommend that negotiations stop completely, however. Rather, it stated "[I]t appears advisable to keep all avenues for negotiation open first because of major military and political implications involved and also because of the possibility of effecting the rescue of a substantial number of Jews."[14]

John Pehle and other WRB members recognized the importance of any offer for Jewish rescue, though they also thought the Nazis might have ulterior motives for supporting the Brand proposal. The WRB sent its field representative Ira Hirschmann, who had worked on rescuing Jews from Turkey, to interview Brand. The Board wanted Hirschmann to determine Brand's trustworthiness and to establish if the proposal was genuine. Before Hirschmann left Washington, FDR instructed him to "Keep talking. Cable back everything you hear. While you talk, these people still have a chance to live."[15] When Hirschmann arrived in Turkey, he learned that British Intelligence had sent Brand to Cairo due to fears about the Nazis' intentions. Hirschmann, determined to carry out his mission, traveled to Cairo

---

13   Ibid.
14   Ibid.
15   Ira Hirschmann, *Caution to the Winds* (New York: D. McKay Co., 1962), 172.

where he finally spoke with Brand.

During the interview Hirschmann asked Brand whether he thought the Nazis would keep their side of the bargain and release Jews. Brand answered yes for two reasons. First of all, once Germany began losing the war, certain items were in short supply, and the Nazis may indeed have been willing to let some Jews go in order to acquire goods or money for themselves. As Brand said to Hirschmann, "I know they need things. I know from years of work that every one of them [the Nazis] can be bought."[16] Secondly, Brand thought the Nazis may have been looking for a way to escape punishment for their persecution of the Jews, in the aftermath of the war. He told Hirschmann, "I can imagine them saying quite brutally, well you [the Allies] have had eight million Jews, we have killed more than six million, we will give you the rest if you do not punish us for killing the others."[17]

From the beginning of negotiations, Brand knew the potential dangers to himself and others that lay in trying to make deals with Nazi leaders. As he told Hirschmann, however, Brand and his organization concluded that "there was no other way outside the illegal way which we were already doing to try to help these people [the Jews]."[18] While the Nazi leaders Brand spoke with did not give him a deadline, Brand's inability to return to them with an offer from the Allies worried him. When Hirschmann interviewed him, he wondered why Brand seemed so pessimistic. Brand had good reason to feel this way. First, deportations of Hungarian Jews had not stopped while he was in Turkey. Tens of thousands per day were packed into rail cars and sent to Auschwitz and Birkenau. Since he had not returned to Istanbul with an offer from the Allies, Brand had even more to worry about. He was afraid for his family's safety and spoke of his fear of an increased number of executions and

---

16   Interrogation of Mr. Joel Brand by Mr. Ira Hirschmann, 22 June 1944, Papers of the War Refugee Board.

17   Ibid.

18   Ibid.

deportations in Hungary.[19] However, he never indicated in the interview that he regretted his efforts to spare the Jews from further suffering.

Hirschmann left the interview convinced that Brand honestly wanted to help Europe's Jews and that the offer to exchange Jews for goods was genuine. He also recommended that negotiations be moved to a neutral country with no British influence.[20] After hearing from their representative, Morgenthau and Pehle, with the approval of President Roosevelt, supported continuing the negotiations. At the very least they thought the offer should not be rejected outright, in the hope that it might lead to other offers.[21] Pleas from Jewish leaders to accept the proposal also poured into the State Department. Some leaders even managed to meet with Secretary Hull, who professed sympathy for the Jews but "expressed serious misgivings regarding any proposal of negotiations."[22] While Jewish leaders understood that the Nazis might have ulterior motives for letting the Jews go, they saw this as a minor issue compared to the 400,000 Jews already deported to death camps such as Birkenau, where tens of thousands died each day. Once again the State Department refused to act independently without consulting the British and the Soviets. Instead, the department sent a cable to Moscow asking for the Soviet government's opinion.[23]

In contrast to the WRB the British and Soviets refused to consider the Brand proposal. A memo from Secretary of State Hull to the American Embassy in Turkey revealed that the Soviet government deemed negotiations with the Germans "neither wise or allowable."[24] Both Britain and the Soviet Union rejected the Brand proposal because of fears that the Germans wanted to divide the

---

19   Ibid.

20   Hirschmann, 175.

21   Wyman, *The Abandonment*, 244.

22   Memo from Shertok for Goldman (World Jewish Congress), 8 July 1944, Papers of the War Refugee Board.

23   Ibid.

24   Paraphrase of telegram sent from secretary of state, Washington, to American Embassy, Ankara, 20 June 1944, Papers of the War Refugee Board.

Allies. The Soviets worried that the trucks the Nazis wanted could be used against them on the Eastern Front. Without the support of Britain and the Soviet Union, the WRB could not provide Brand with an Allied response to the proposal and he never returned to Istanbul to make a deal with the Nazi leadership. As a result, the deportations of Hungarian Jewry continued. In this case, the desire of the WRB and the president to keep negotiations going was hampered by America's allies. Nevertheless, the WRB, unlike the British and Soviets, did not completely give up on the Brand proposal; instead it followed Hirschmann's advice and pursued the matter in the neutral country of Switzerland.

However, in the following instance, even the WRB's response to a rescue proposal was limited and inadequate. In August 1944 Saly Mayer, a Swiss representative of the American Jewish Joint Distribution Committee (JDC), began negotiations with three German agents. Mayer wanted to strike a bargain for the Jews still in Budapest. The instructions Mayer received from Washington hardly encouraged negotiations, however. In a memo to the under secretary of state, Pehle wrote that while "the War Refugee Board would favor any time-gaining device," he felt that "we [the United States] can not enter into any ransom transactions with the German authorities to obtain the release of Jews."[25] The Germans with whom Mayer met also made his efforts more difficult. Instead of money, they asked for trucks. As usual, the Allies worried that these materials would be used against them in the war. Mayer pointed this out to the Germans and tried to steer the conversation to money instead, even though he knew the Allies would give him nothing.[26] The WRB was limited by the insistence of its own members and the Roosevelt administration to keep Allied goods and capital from the Nazis.

The WRB's stance was unfortunate because of a recent split in the Nazi ranks over Hitler's Jewish policies. From his initial meeting,

25   Memo from Mr. Pehle to Mr. Stettinius, 17 August 1944, Papers of the War Refugee Board.

26   Paraphrase of telegram received from American Legation Bern to secretary of state, Washington, 26 August 1944, Papers of the War Refugee Board.

Mayer learned that two out of three Nazi factions expressed either indifference to or dislike of the Final Solution.[27] This indicated that the Nazis could indeed be bought, but the Allies paid no attention. Mayer still had reason to feel hopeful about aiding at least some Jews, however. As a result of his meeting with the German agents, more than three hundred Hungarian Jews arrived in Switzerland from the Bergen-Belsen concentration camp, and the American Legation in Switzerland expected the arrival of a further two hundred Jews.[28] The release of the Bergen-Belsen Jews demonstrated that the Germans took their negotiations with Mayer seriously.

Shortly after the initial group of Jews arrived in Switzerland, the Nazis changed their ransom demands from goods to money. Specifically they offered to set free all Hungarian Jews if Mayer procured $50,000,000.[29] Mayer managed to stall them and arrange a later meeting without committing himself. He did get a commitment from the Nazis, though. Mayer requested that another 1,400 Jews from Bergen-Belsen be sent to Switzerland.[30] Once again, the Nazis complied and demonstrated their willingness to get rid of Jews via negotiations with the Allies when given the opportunity. If more than a thousand Jewish men, women and children were freed without any conditions, one can only imagine how many Jews Mayer might have rescued if the Allies had provided him with goods or cash.

Even though the Allies were clearly winning the war, the fear of potentially helping the Nazis fight back by giving them money persisted. Despite these constraints the WRB offered some help to Mayer. Understandably Mayer felt he needed some evidence to show the Germans that the Allies supported his efforts to save Hungarian Jews so the supposed negotiations could continue. By

---

27   Ibid.

28   Ibid.

29   Telegram from Lisbon Embassy to Leavitt at WRB, 28 August 1944, Papers of the War Refugee Board.

30   Ibid.

fall of 1944 an exhausted Mayer was convinced that the Germans had lost patience with his stalling and that any further negotiations would be useless.[31] At this point John Pehle played a crucial role in keeping the talks between Mayer and the Germans alive. Under Pehle's instructions, the WRB eventually granted a deposit of 20,000,000 Swiss francs from the JDC (the equivalent of $5 million) in blocked accounts to bolster Mayer's credibility.[32] Mayer could not actually use this money, however. The WRB made it clear that "the transfer has been approved solely in order that Saly Mayer may have something tangible with which to hold open the negotiations and for the gaining of more precious time."[33] Time was all Mayer could hope to win, since he was not permitted to pay a ransom for Hungarian Jews.

The Board offered two reasons for not allowing Mayer to use the funds. First, they needed permission from the Allies to spend the money.[34] Technically this was untrue, as the money came from a private organization, not the United States government. That is not to say that the Allies would have wanted America to act alone; on the contrary, the Soviet Union and Britain made it clear during the Brand negotiations that they disapproved of the United States paying for Jewish lives.

Even if one buys the Board's reasoning that it needed to keep its allies happy during a time of war, the second excuse is more difficult to believe. The Board stated in an earlier memo to its representative in Switzerland, "[W]e are not at all convinced that large monetary payments to the German government would be successful."[35] How did the Board know that payments would be unsuccessful if such measures were never tried? WRB members already knew of Brand's opinion that the Nazis could be bought, an opinion based on years

---

31 Telegram from American Legation, Bern to secretary of state, Washington, 16 September 1944, Papers of the War Refugee Board.

32 Department of State outgoing telegram to Bern for McClelland from Department and WRB, 6 January 1945, Papers of the War Refugee Board.

33 Ibid.

34 Ibid.

35 Telegram from secretary of state, Washington, and WRB to American Legation, Bern and McClelland, 30 August 1944, Papers of the War Refugee Board.

of experience in dealing with the Germans. The Allies also had first-hand accounts of ransom negotiations that had taken place within the concentration camps. In October 1944 Jan Karski, a member of the Polish underground, disguised himself as a guard at a Belzec death camp and reported his findings to the Allies. Karski's Estonian guide, who was also a guard, told him, "We do business with people on the outside, like you. If somebody comes to me and tells me that such and such a Jew is going to arrive and that he wants him 'cheated out'—well if he is willing to fork out plenty of hard cash in advance, then I do what I can."[36] Though such transactions were carried out on a smaller scale than other offers discussed in this chapter, they substantiate Brand's belief that at least some members of the Nazi machine allowed Jewish rescue when it was to their advantage. Mayer's first meeting with German agents further demonstrated that divisions existed among the Nazis. These favorable conditions, combined with the fact that the Allies were winning the war, make Allied reluctance to ransom at least some Jews seem unconscionable.

Even without much support from the Allies, Mayer's adroit negotiating skills produced concrete results. The talks led to the release of 1,673 Hungarian Jews from Bergen-Belsen. They were released to show the power and influence of the German negotiators and to prove that the offer was genuine. An additional 17,000 Jews were also saved because the Nazis anticipated their release under the negotiations with Mayer.[37] The saving of these lives under such strict conditions makes one wonder how many more lives might have been saved if the Mayer negotiations and other Nazi proposals were fully exploited. Although there is no way to know exactly how many Jews could have escaped under the various ransom proposals or which offers would have proved successful, the reluctance of the Allies to supply the Nazis with Allied goods should have been overridden by the desire to preserve human lives.

---

36   Jan Karski, "Polish Death Camp," *Collier's*, 14 October 1944. Reprinted in *America Views the Holocaust, 1933–1945: A Brief Documentary History*, ed. Robert Abzug (Boston and New York: Bedford/St. Martin's, 1999), 185.

37   Morse, 300.

CHAPTER SIX

A New Kind of Warfare: The WRB's Use of Propaganda and Threats

IN ADDITION TO FACILITATING RANSOM proposals, the War Refugee Board's rescue efforts involved other methods of aid. One method, known as psychological warfare, was used often throughout the spring and summer of 1944. Psychological warfare involved issuing threats of postwar punishment to the Nazis and their satellites for their mistreatment of Jews. Since Hungary was surrounded by Nazi-controlled territory, direct rescue of Jews was difficult. Instead, the Board hoped to stop deportations by putting psychological pressure on government officials as well as the people of Hungary. A statement known as the Moscow Declaration, signed by President Roosevelt, Winston Churchill, and Joseph Stalin, was put in force in November 1943.[1] Although the declaration warned of future punishment for atrocities and executions committed by the Nazis, it failed to specifically mention Jews.

Board members wanted European countries to know without any doubt that mistreatment of Jews was unacceptable to the United States. At the Board's request, Under Secretary of State Stettinius sent a message to the American legation in Bern. The legation was told to contact the governments of Bulgaria, Rumania, and Hungary and to inform them that the United States viewed any mistreatment of Jews in those countries with "great seriousness."[2] Though the

---

1   *Final Summary Report of the Executive Director, War Refugee Board*, 15 September 1945, Papers of the War Refugee Board.

2   Paraphrase of telegram sent from secretary of state, Washington, to American Legation, Bern, 7 March 1944, Papers of the War Refugee Board.

memo specifically mentioned the Jews, the punishment for those who persecuted them remained vague. The United States had always officially disagreed with Nazi persecution of minorities. The question was what, if anything, would the Allies do to the perpetrators once the war was over?

Pehle and other members of the WRB pushed for a new US declaration that emphasized the murder of Jews and the retribution the Nazis and others could expect from the Allies for such crimes. For such an important announcement, they needed the backing of the president. Preferably, the president would issue the declaration himself, thus adding teeth to the threats against the Nazis and their satellites. Members of the WRB drafted a declaration for FDR to broadcast in March. The original draft referred to the Jews in the very first sentence. It stated, "One of the blackest crimes in history, the systematic murder of the Jews in Europe, continues unabated."[3] The statement went on to emphasize that anyone, regardless of their authority or lack thereof, who assisted in the deportation of Jews to the death camps could expect postwar punishment.[4] The emphasis on the mistreatment of Jews in a presidential statement was unprecedented, but the Board thought it was appropriate considering that the Nazi extermination policy primarily focused on the Jews. When the president read the Board's draft, however, he refused to issue it. FDR indicated to his cabinet that "the declaration referred to the atrocities against the Jews in too pointed a manner."[5] He may have worried that anti-Semitic feeling in the United States ran too high for him to issue such a strong statement against the mistreatment of Jews while his country was at war. He certainly did not want to lose support for the war effort, and he was, as always, concerned for his own popularity. Even as Allied forces closed in on the Nazis, the president of the United States hesitated to mention the suffering of the Jews in a public speech.

---

3   Original draft for 20 March 1944 message, Papers of the War Refugee Board.
4   Ibid.
5   John Pehle, memorandum for the files, 9 March 1944, Papers of the War Refugee Board.

Worried that the president would not issue any declaration on Nazi war crimes, John Pehle agreed to move the statement on crimes against the Jews from the first paragraph to the fourth. Despite the changes to the declaration, FDR needed further convincing to endorse it. The task of persuading the president went to his old friend Henry Morgenthau. Pehle asked Morgenthau to emphasize the importance of the message prior to his meeting with FDR. Pehle told Morgenthau, "The statement is badly needed" for the Board's psychological warfare campaign and that "although some of us would have preferred the statement in its earlier form we are all agreed that even as amended it will be helpful and are anxious to get it out promptly."[6] In other words, some mention of Jewish persecution and subsequent punishment for those who participated in it was better than no mention at all. Evidently the meeting between the two friends went well, as the president agreed to issue the new statement on March 24, 1944.

FDR's broadcast kept some of the wording from the original WRB draft. It still referred to the murder of the Jews as "one of the blackest crimes of all history" and further warned that those who helped to deport Jews from Hungary would suffer punishment after the war.[7] Unlike the first draft, however, FDR's statement did not open with the condemnation of those who persecuted Jews. In fact the first two paragraphs failed to mention Jews at all while listing almost every other group the Nazis mistreated but were not in the habit of exterminating. Listeners to the broadcast could infer that Jews were among the "many others" subjugated by the Nazis, but the president did not actually use the word Jew until the fourth paragraph of his speech.[8] Still, any condemnation of the Jewish genocide was a remarkable departure from FDR's usual circumspect treatment of the issue. His assertion that anyone who took part in deporting or otherwise mistreating Jews would be held accountable to the

---

6   John Pehle to Secretary Morgenthau, 16 March 1944, Papers of the War Refugee Board.

7   Extract of President Roosevelt's statement of March 24, 1944, Papers of the War Refugee Board.

8   Ibid.

United Nations after the war was unprecedented. In paragraph five FDR stated, "All who knowingly take part in the deportation of Jews to their death in Poland or Norwegians and French to their death in Germany are equally guilty with the executioner."[9] The WRB's original draft referred to Jews only; the French and Norwegians were likely added to deflect some attention from the Jews. Notwithstanding the statement's limitations, the members of the War Refugee Board had managed to convince the leader of the free world to issue the first direct warning to the persecutors of Europe's Jews.

Once FDR issued his statement, the WRB ensured that it was conveyed by every possible means. The Office of War Information (OWI) gave the statement "heavy play in all major languages" multiple times from its New York office.[10] For example, the complete text was played in French three times and was referred to in forty broadcasts.[11] The statement was also referenced in German in fifty-one broadcasts between March 24 and March 25.[12] Despite the OWI's extensive coverage of the declaration, the complete text was not played each time. Therefore, it is difficult to determine which parts of the statement were emphasized. The OWI's San Francisco office reported "playing up the refugee passages, thirty times in seven languages."[13] Unfortunately, the foreign languages broadcast from San Francisco, with the exception of French, were Oriental rather than European.

The War Refugee Board used other methods besides radio broadcasts to deliver the president's message. American newspapers like the *New York Times* printed the full text of the message. In case the Nazis or their satellite countries happened to miss the OWI

---

9   Ibid.

10   Broadcasts from New York: OWI's Use of President's Refugee Statement in OWI Broadcasts, 27 March 1944, Papers of the War Refugee Board.

11   Ibid.

12   Ibid.

13   Broadcasts from San Francisco: Use of President's Refugee Statement in OWI Broadcasts, 29 March 1944, Papers of the War Refugee Board.

broadcasts, the WRB ensured that underground publications in Europe had access to the statement.[14] If the Nazis still harbored doubts about the United States' commitment to punishing murderers of the Jews, the message was also conveyed by Allied planes, which dropped leaflets containing the president's message over Nazi-controlled territories, including Hungary.[15]

Even the British government, though not always supportive of the WRB's activities, decided to support the president's declaration. The British Embassy told the American ambassador, "We fully share the President's view of the importance of the psychological warfare value of his declaration."[16] The British not only supported the president's March 24 statement, but British Secretary of State Anthony Eden made a similar declaration in the House of Commons on March 30. Eden's statement confirmed the determination of the Allies that those responsible for murdering Jews would be brought to justice. Like FDR's declaration, Eden's statement was broadcast in multiple foreign languages.[17]

During the next month, the War Refugee Board needed all the support it could muster as the Nazis pressured the Hungarian people to help them deport Jews. At first the Board only requested its foreign ministers to remind Hungarians that "any action on the part of the Hungarian government to inflict new and further persecutions ... against foreign or native Jews" would be looked upon in the United States "with the greatest disfavor and will be taken into account after the war."[18] Yet members of the Board soon realized that reminders of the president's March 24 statement were inadequate. In early April Gerhart Riegner telegraphed Stephen Wise to say he had reliable

---

14   *Final Summary Report of the Executive Director, War Refugee Board,* 15 September 1945, Papers of the War Refugee Board.

15   Ibid.

16   Ambassador Winant, telegram to secretary of state, Washington, from London, 6 April 1944, Papers of the War Refugee Board.

17   Ibid.

18   Telegram sent to American Legation, Lisbon from secretary of state, Washington, 12 April 1944, Papers of the War Refugee Board.

reports that the Nazis planned to exterminate Hungarian Jews.[19] The Nazis believed that Hungarians would help them deport the remaining Jews to concentration camps. As a result the WRB needed to respond to the crisis with equal determination.

Throughout the spring of 1944, the WRB issued pleas, statements, and direct threats from a variety of sources in an effort to influence Hungarians. Almost on a daily basis, the Office of War Information broadcast statements from former Hungarian officials, United States senators, and church leaders, who urged Hungarians not to comply with Nazi demands. In April an American Catholic priest of Hungarian heritage called upon his former countrymen to protect Jews and defy the people who had conquered their country. The broadcast "caused a furor within Hungary" and even prompted the Hungarian Nazi press to rebut the statement.[20] Since the Nazi press generally ignored criticism, the priest's message must have made some Hungarians reconsider their decision to aid the Nazi cause.

By late April it appeared that at least some Hungarians rejected the Nazi propaganda that the Jews were responsible for everything negative that happened in Hungary during World War II. In a message to the people of Hungary, the United States government recognized that Hungarians still shopped in Jewish stores and that some even tried to help Jews keep their property. The United States asked Hungarians to increase the amount of help they gave to the Jews in their communities. Hungarians were reminded of FDR's words of March 24: "I ask every man everywhere under Nazi domination to show the world by his action that in his heart he does not share Hitler's insane criminal desires. Let him hide these pursued victims, help them get over their borders and do what he can to save them from the Nazi hangman."[21]

---

19   Wyman, *The Abandonment*, 236.
20   Memorandum: Hungarian language radio broadcasts relating to refugees, 15 May 1944, Papers of the War Refugee Board.
21   Text of US appeal to Hungarians to aid Hungarian Jews, Released 26 April 1944, Papers of the War Refugee Board.

Despite the warnings, deportations of Hungarian Jews began in May, causing the WRB to try additional means of influencing Hungary's population as well as Nazi officials. The WRB urged neutral countries and the International Committee of the Red Cross to assign further representatives to Hungary in the hope that more observers would lessen the number of deportations. Sweden and the ICRC responded to pressure from the Board. Sweden sent a direct appeal to Hungary, and the ICRC eventually sent a message to Horthy that requested detailed information on deported Jews.[22] The WRB's *Final Summary Report* stated that the presence of neutral officials helped to save people from death or deportation.[23] No concrete numbers of Jews saved by this tactic exist, but as Joel Brand noted, not all Nazi leaders agreed with Hitler that the extermination of Jews should take priority even if the Germans were losing the war. The division among the Nazis on the Jewish question may have caused some to be more inclined to heed officials from the Red Cross and elsewhere.

In addition to approaching neutrals and the ICRC, the War Refugee Board pressured the people of Hungary to listen to their spiritual leaders. As the appeal by a priest of Hungarian descent to a largely Catholic country proved successful in the spring, the WRB requested additional cooperation from church leaders. For example, the Vatican was urged to speak out against Nazi atrocities. On June 25 Pope Pius XII telegraphed a personal appeal to Miklós Horthy.[24] Many other church leaders agreed to contribute broadcasts denouncing the Nazi treatment of the Jews. In addition to the Pope, Archbishop Francis Spellman of New York told Hungarians that the persecution of the Jews contradicted Catholic doctrine.[25] The Office of War Information broadcast his appeal five

---

22 Wyman, *The Abandonment*, 238.
23 *Final Summary Report of the Executive Director, War Refugee Board*, 15 September 1945, Papers of the War Refugee Board.
24 Wyman, *The Abandonment*, 238.
25 Office of War Information memo, subject: Hungarian scripts, 19 July 1944, Papers of the War Refugee Board.

times from June 29 to July 2. Other religious leaders, including the Archbishop of Canterbury, the Zurich Council of Churches, and a group of German Catholic bishops condemned the persecution of people based on their ethnicity.[26] Considering that the Catholic Church had done little to protest the Jewish slaughter up to this point, the WRB's success in convincing church officials to help was remarkable.

In addition to the Catholic Church, the WRB's psychological warfare campaign also influenced foreign countries. An underground radio station in Russia, Radio Kossuth, began broadcasting protests against Jewish persecution in July 1944. The broadcast urged Hungarians to aid Jews and encouraged Jews either to attempt escape or to join Resistance groups.[27] Though not an official Russian radio station, Radio Kossuth demonstrated that once the United States announced its displeasure over the mistreatment of Jews, other countries would follow that example.

After months of asking politicians and church groups to contribute to the War Refugee Board's psychological warfare campaign, its executive director finally received some good news. On August 11 a telegram arrived for John Pehle from WRB representative Ira Hirschmann. It stated, "[I]t has been reported to us through reliable sources out of Hungary that the warning transmitted by radio to the Hungarians emanating from the Board has had a salutary effect . . . it is reported that the Hungarians are beginning to show some signs of resistance to the Germans."[28] Hirschmann added that further warnings should be sent. The effect of psychological pressure on the people of Hungary remains difficult to quantify, but at the very least the Board's messages persuaded some people not to contribute to the Jews' suffering.

Indeed, the psychological warfare initiated by the WRB affected Hungarian officials during the summer of 1944. The *Final Summary*

---

26 Ibid.

27 Ibid.

28 Incoming telegram for Pehle from Hirschmann Ankara No. 130, 11 August 1944, Papers of the War Refugee Board.

Report of the Executive Director states that the many warnings to
Hungarian officials sent by the United States and other democracies
led to Miklós Horthy's suggestion that those democracies take in
Hungary's Jews.[29] A German newspaper article from August 1944
supported the WRB's statement. The article stated, "Pressure from
the enemy and neutral countries has become so strong that those
circles in Hungary that are friendly to the Jews ... influence the
Hungarian government to prevent any further measures against the
Jews."[30] Nevertheless, psychological pressure, though a powerful
motivator in the Horthy offer, could not alone save the Jews of
Hungary. Cooperation between Britain and the United States,
both of whom were named in the offer, was needed to support the
WRB's psychological warfare campaign. Unfortunately the efforts
of the WRB failed to save Jews under Horthy's offer because the
United States and British governments failed to cooperate quickly
enough.

Although they experienced some failures as well as some
successes, the members of the WRB refused to cease their campaign
of psychological warfare. In fact the campaign intensified as the
war came to an end because of reports that "a last minute orgy
of Jews" would take place.[31] In 1945 William O'Dwyer, who
later became mayor of New York City, was appointed as the new
director of the WRB. John Pehle had left his post to take another
position in the Treasury Department in the belief that most of
the WRB's work was complete. Though not as familiar with the
workings of the WRB as Pehle, O'Dwyer saw that more warnings
needed to be sent to all Germans—not just the Nazis—who might
take the frustration of their military losses out on the Jews who
were awaiting rescue by Allied forces. O'Dwyer prodded the State
Department to issue a new statement indicating that the United

---

29   *Final Summary Report of the Executive Director, War Refugee Board*, 15 September 1945,
       Papers of the War Refugee Board.
30   Feingold, 269.
31   Memo from William O'Dwyer to secretary of state, 6 April 1945, Papers of the War
       Refugee Board.

States considered any method of murder by individuals or groups against Jews worthy of postwar punishment.[32]

On April 23, 1945 a statement was issued not only by the United States but also by Great Britain and the Soviet Union. It warned that any German guilty of maltreating civilian detainees would be "ruthlessly pursued and brought to punishment."[33] Finally, the WRB brought all the Allies, including the Soviet Union, together in an official statement against Nazi atrocities against Jews. The *Final Summary Report of the Executive Director* referred to the statement as "the strongest formal threat" issued by the Allies before the end of the war.[34]

The statement, though powerful and likely responsible for saving some Jews, came late. Millions of Jews had already been murdered before the Allies made a joint declaration on postwar punishment for the Nazis and their followers. The War Refugee Board, however, did its best throughout 1944 to issue any statements on postwar punishment for the mistreatment of minorities that the United States government and its allies allowed. Sadly, the Board often dealt with the reluctance of political leaders to mention the Jews directly in their statements, thus making its efforts at psychological warfare less effective than they might otherwise have been.

---

32   Ibid.
33   Ibid.
34   *Final Summary Report of the Executive Director, War Refugee Board*, 15 September 1945, Papers of the War Refugee Board.

CHAPTER SEVEN

The WRB in Turkey: The Accomplishments of Field Representative Ira Hirschmann

IN ADDITION TO ISSUING THREATS and warnings from the United States, John Pehle decided to appoint representatives of the Board in several neutral countries. Pehle used the power vested in him by the executive order, which stated that special attachés could be assigned to implement the Board's policies in other countries. He asked Ira Hirschmann, the vice-president of Bloomingdale's department store, to represent the WRB in Turkey.[1] Although sometimes criticized for his lack of diplomatic experience, Hirschmann showed concern for the plight of Jews long before his appointment. Prior to receiving his assignment from the WRB, he served as chairman of the board for the University in Exile, which offered haven and teaching positions to scholars forced from their homelands by Hitler. The experience made Hirschmann "unalterably committed to the absolute necessity of saving the lives of victims of Nazism."[2] The Board's appointment gave him much more power to facilitate rescue and provide aid for refugees. As a neutral country surrounded by Axis territory, Turkey was a potential place of refuge for fleeing Jews, especially since its waterways and rail routes connected to Palestine.

After accepting his post, Hirschmann focused on opening a

---

1   Telegram to American Embassy, Ankara from State Department, 12 February 1944, Papers of the War Refugee Board.

2   Hirschmann, 101.

sea route from Rumania, which was a Nazi-occupied territory. He hoped to obtain temporary use of Turkish ships, which would bring Rumanian Jews to Turkey. The British government agreed to allow into Palestine refugees who reached Turkey, a fact John Pehle hoped would calm Turkey's concerns about being inundated with refugees.[3] Furthermore the United States promised to provide food and to pay for the needs of refugees during their short stay in Turkey.[4]

The cooperation of the British government in aiding refugees who arrived in Turkey was a relatively recent development. In 1942, 769 Jews fled Rumania for Palestine. Crowded into a small ship named the *Struma*, they landed in Turkey following the failure of the ship's engine. The Turks wanted assurance that any refugees they took in could go to Palestine, but the British refused to provide this guarantee. As a result the Turkish government insisted on the removal of the ship, which was torpedoed, leaving just one survivor.[5] After a public outcry, the British altered their strict immigration stance and stated that Jews who arrived in Turkey could proceed to Palestine. Turkey, in turn, ended its total rejection of refugees.[6]

In 1944, with the promise of British assistance and the aid of American Ambassador Laurence Steinhardt, Hirschmann entered into negotiations with the Turkish government to acquire the necessary ships. The WRB's hopes for cooperation from the Turkish authorities soon turned to frustration. In February 1944 the Turkish ship SS *Vatan*, which had the capacity to transfer 800 refugees out of Rumania, caught Hirschmann's attention; however, the local government continued to find reasons to delay its use. First, Turkish authorities insisted that the United States replace the ship if it was lost at sea. After learning of their demands, Pehle wasted no time contacting the head of the War Shipping Administration in Washington, who promised that if the

---

3   Telegram sent to American Embassy, Ankara from secretary of state, Washington, 26 February 1944, Papers of the War Refugee Board.

4   War Refugee Board internal memo, no date, Papers of the War Refugee Board.

5   Wyman, *The Abandonment*, 158.

6   Ibid., 159.

SS *Vatan* were lost, the Administration would replace it.[7] Still the Turkish government withheld permission to use the ship. A WRB memo stated that "Finally on March 4, after weeks of delay, the Foreign Office advised Ambassador Steinhardt that the immediate charter of the SS VATAN for a single voyage from Constanza was approved in principle by the Foreign Office ... however, the charter was never authorized."[8] The failure to secure the use of the ship hurt Jewish rescue efforts in the Balkans, because it had the capacity to transfer a large number of passengers in a single voyage.

Despite the SS *Vatan* fiasco, Steinhardt and Hirschmann continued to negotiate with the Turkish government. In mid-March, Steinhardt received an offer from the Turkish foreign minister, which stated that the government would make a passenger ship available for voyages to Rumania and back. The offer again contained one caveat: that the United States government promise to provide a replacement vessel in case the ship, named the SS *Tari*, was lost at sea. Otherwise, the *Tari*, which had the capacity to carry over 1,000 refugees, would make just one trip.[9] Some time was wasted as Secretary Morgenthau tried to convince Admiral Land to guarantee replacement of the SS *Tari*. Land and the WRB expressed frustration that the Turks insisted on a replacement passenger vessel when in fact the SS *Tari* was a freighter that had been converted into a passenger ship.[10] Moreover, passenger ships were difficult to come by during the war. Because of this, Land offered the Turkish government only a replacement cargo vessel.[11] Yet the WRB did not want to limit the SS *Tari* to just one voyage when thousands of refugees could potentially be saved with multiple trips. The WRB tried to strike a compromise, and stated

7   Letter to John Pehle from E. S. Land, Administrator War Shipping Administration, Washington, 23 February 1944, Papers of the War Refugee Board.
8   War Refugee Board internal memo, no date, Papers of the War Refugee Board.
9   Paraphrase of telegram sent to London Embassy from secretary of state, Washington: War Refugee Board sends the following for Ambassador Winant, 31 March 1944, Papers of the War Refugee Board.
10 Treasury Department inter-office communication to Mr. Pehle from Mr. Friedman, 23 March 1944, Papers of the War Refugee Board.
11 War Refugee Board internal memo, no date, Papers of the War Refugee Board.

that, "If necessary, the War Refugee Board will also assume responsibility for financing the conversion of such a cargo ship into a passenger ship of the general character of the SS TARI."[12]

Nevertheless, as in the case of the SS *Vatan*, as soon as one demand was met, the Turks came up with another. Although they had assurance that the SS *Tari* would be replaced if necessary, Turkish authorities also wanted assurances from all of the Axis powers that the vessel would be allowed safe passage. Hirschmann and the WRB had little if any control over other countries that might care nothing about the fate of Jewish refugees. Amazingly, most belligerent countries promised not to harm the SS *Tari*, but Germany remained the exception. Hirschmann and Steinhardt reported to Pehle, "[W]e invite the attention of the Board to the fact that we have now taken every step which it is within our power to take to obtain the German safe conduct. As the representative of the International Red Cross in Ankara informs us ... that there will be considerable delay in obtaining the German safe conduct and as the TARI which will be prepared to sail within a week, will not be permitted to depart until the German safe conduct is forthcoming, we urge the Board to exert every possible effort towards expediting the German safe conduct."[13] Once again the WRB used psychological warfare in an attempt to influence the Germans. The WRB contacted other governments, including those of Sweden and Switzerland, who agreed to pressure Germany to let Rumanian refugees depart in safety.[14] In addition, branches of the International Red Cross, and even the Pope requested safe conduct for the SS *Tari*.[15]

The Board's psychological warfare campaign continued for months. In the meantime, however, relations between Turkey

---

12   Ibid.

13   Telegram from the ambassador and Hirschmann for the WRB, 27 March 1944, Papers of the War Refugee Board.

14   Paraphrase of telegram received from Ankara Embassy to secretary of state, Washington, 2 May 1944, Papers of the War Refugee Board.

15   Ibid.

and Germany soured. Steinhardt reported to the WRB in May that Turkey had abruptly stopped sending chrome shipments to Germany, which made guarantees of safe conduct for the SS *Tari* improbable.[16] Whether the Turks deliberately antagonized the Germans in order to avoid the use of their ships in the Board's Jewish rescue efforts cannot be proven. Considering its lack of interest in helping refugees, however, the Turkish government was likely pleased that it did not have to help the WRB.

In addition to its reluctance to donate ships, the Turks also delayed the process of issuing Turkish transit visas to refugees, thus preventing them from entering Turkey. Hirschmann and Steinhardt were assured in March that Rumanian refugees could pass through Turkey in two groups of seventy-five every ten days.[17] Some refugees arrived safely in Turkey, but Hirschmann's assumption that "the stoppage in refugee movement through Turkey which had existed since the first of January has been overcome" proved inaccurate.[18] In reality the Turks continued to delay the issuing of visas. Therefore, if a refugee managed to reach Turkey, border guards might still turn him or her away. Even if a refugee was approved for a visa, he or she often had to give *baksheesh*—a bribe—to a Turkish official in order to obtain it.[19]

As mentioned above, the British promised to allow Rumanian refugees who reached Turkey to enter into Palestine, so their stay in Turkey would be brief. Furthermore the United States pledged to provide for the refugees during their brief transition period. Since the refugees were not staying, and the Turks did not have to provide them with food, why did the Turkish government hesitate to rescue the Rumanian refugees? The answer was not much

---

16 Ibid.
17 Paraphrase of telegram received from American Embassy, Ankara to secretary of state, Washington: Following for Pehle from Hirschmann, 4 March 1944, Papers of the War Refugee Board.
18 Ibid.
19 Treasury Department Inter Office Communication to Mr. Friedman from Mr. Marks, 5 April 1944, Papers of the War Refugee Board.

different from the excuses the United States State Department gave for refusing to admit refugees in 1943. Like the State Department, the Turkish government used security concerns as an excuse. As the Treasury Department noted, "[V]aluable time (two or three weeks) could be saved if the Turkish government automatically granted Turkish transit visas to refugees showing evidence of having been granted entry to Palestine. The Turkish objection to this would be primarily on security grounds. However Turkish security would not be endangered if refugees … were kept under strict surveillance."[20] Like the State Department, the Turks worried that spies or other undesirable persons would enter their country, so they either took extra time issuing visas, or flatly refused to provide refugees with visas. In retrospect the United States' criticism of Turkey's visa policies was hypocritical, as the State Department did everything possible to prevent Jewish refugees from coming to America.

In the midst of negotiations for Turkish ships and transit visas, the WRB continued to look for ways to get Jewish refugees out of the Balkans. The agency located three Bulgarian boats named the SS *Milka*, *Maritza*, and *Bellacitta*, which the Bulgarian authorities agreed to hire out for high rates.[21] None of the Bulgarian ships were great alternatives to the SS *Vatan* or the *Tari*. Each Bulgarian vessel carried fewer than half the passengers of the Turkish ships. Most importantly, the International Red Cross had previously declared both the *Milka* and the *Maritza* unseaworthy.[22] Yet the Turks would not give their ships up for rescue purposes. Likewise, the WRB was determined not to give up on the possibility of rescuing refugees. Despite the expense and risks involved, the War Refugee Board and the American Jewish Joint Distribution Committee hired the Bulgarian boats.[23]

Early on, the Bulgarian boats successfully brought refugees from

---

20   Ibid.

21   Wyman, *The Abandonment*, 218.

22   Treasury Department Inter Office Communication to Mr. Friedman from Mr. Marks, 5 April 1944, Papers of the War Refugee Board.

23   Wyman, *The Abandonment*, 217–18.

Rumania to Turkey. During the course of two voyages in April, the SS *Milka* carried a total of 511 refugees. Initially, the Turkish Foreign Office refused to let the *Milka* land. Determined to save the refugees, Hirschmann pressured Steinhardt to persuade the Turkish government to make an exception. The Turkish foreign minister reluctantly agreed. Overjoyed, Hirschmann watched the *Milka*'s passengers disembark and transfer to the railcars that would bring them to freedom in Palestine.[24] After the *Milka* landed on Turkish shores, other ships followed. The SS *Maritza* brought in 244 refugees and the SS *Bellacitta* rescued 152.[25] Pehle noted, "[D]uring the month of April a total of 907 refugees were evacuated from Constanza to Turkey on these small boats. All of the rescued people have been permitted transit through Turkey to Palestine."[26] Compared to the number of Jews who could have been saved by Turkish ships, the success of these rescue missions appeared small. In consideration of the difficulties Hirschmann and Steinhardt encountered trying to bring refugees into Turkey, however, any success was significant and commendable.

Though the Turkish police ordered rescue workers not to speak to the refugees as they came off the ships, Hirschmann became acquainted with a Polish Jewish boy named Motek. Back in Poland, Nazis had shot Motek's family members while he hid in a barrel of water. Motek left his village and walked all the way to the Slovakian border, where the underground helped smuggle him into Hungary. He joined a group of children led by a Hungarian underground volunteer who sacrificed her life to bring the children to safety. After his brief stay in Turkey, Motek left for Palestine with the other passengers who had a chance at starting new lives.[27] For refugees like Motek, the Bulgarian boats were a godsend.

In late May, however, an incident occurred that prevented the

---

24   Hirschmann, 142.
25   Memo to Secretary Morgenthau from Pehle, 3 May 1944, Papers of the War Refugee Board.
26   Ibid.
27   Hirschmann, 143.

WRB from using Bulgarian boats for additional rescue missions. The warnings from the Red Cross that the *Maritza* was unsafe proved accurate when it sank in the Black Sea. No refugees were aboard as the ship was returning to Rumania, but as the *New York Daily* reported, "[I]ts loss may strand hundreds of Jews in Rumania."[28] After the ship sank, Bulgaria refused to permit even small ships to be used in rescue missions.

Despite the refusals of the Turkish and Bulgarian authorities to support the WRB's mission, Hirschmann refused to give up. Though the Turks still would not allow large ships to transport refugees, Hirschmann found four small, privately owned merchandise ships whose owners were unconcerned about safe conduct guarantees as long as they were well compensated. In addition, one Greek ship became available. With the exception of the Greek ship, which could hold 1,200 passengers, the ships carried only a few hundred each.[29] Once again, the American Jewish Joint Distribution Committee offered to share the cost of the boats, thus increasing the chances for the WRB to acquire them.

In spite of some transportation limitations, summer negotiations with the Turkish government led to an unprecedented deal. Steinhardt received assurances from the secretary general of the Ministry of Foreign Affairs that passengers could arrive in Turkey without transit visas and still be sent to Palestine.[30] Now Jewish refugees who had no chance of getting into Turkey a few months before were welcomed. The reasons for the Turkish government's change of heart are unclear; however, its actions were likely the result of adroit negotiating by Steinhardt and Hirschmann as well as the Allies' continued progress toward winning the war.

The acquisition of Turkish boats led to the safe arrival of Rumanian refugees in Istanbul. For example, in July the SS *Kazbek* brought

---

28   "Refugee Ship's Sinking May Strand Hundreds," *New York Daily*, 31 May 1944, filed in Papers of the War Refugee Board.

29   Incoming telegram from Ankara to secretary of state, Washington: For WRB from Hirschmann, 5 July 1944, Papers of the War Refugee Board.

30   Ibid.

759 refugees to Turkey, including 265 children.[31] Steinhardt must have made an impression on the Turkish foreign minister, as he kept his word that the refugees would be sent to Palestine after entering Turkey. Ecstatic with the progress made in eliminating red tape for refugees, Hirschmann believed that the deadlock that caused rescue from the Balkans to nearly cease was broken.[32] His prediction was premature. Hirschmann could not foresee the fate of one of the Turkish motorboats, named the *Mefkure*. As the *Mefkure* left Rumania with refugees on board during the night of August 3, German torpedo boats fired on the Turkish ship. The *Mefkure* burst into flames. One hundred children trapped in the ship perished. Most refugees who managed to jump into the water also died as the Germans shot at them.[33] The loss of the *Mefkure* presented the Turks with the ideal excuse to withdraw from a rescue mission they never supported.

The War Refugee Board's efforts to bring Rumanian Jews to Palestine via Turkey had limited success. According to the Board's *Final Summary Report*, nearly 7,000 Jews left the Balkans under Hirschmann's watch.[34] The number saved paled in comparison to the millions who had already died before the WRB and its representatives could take action. Yet every life saved was an accomplishment, especially considering the reluctance of the Turkish authorities to cooperate with any plans to rescue Jews.

Though the WRB initially expected Hirschmann to aid refugees by negotiating with Turkish authorities, Hirschmann's greatest accomplishment as a representative of the WRB stemmed from his negotiations with other foreign ministers. He realized he had to meet with Alexander Cretzianu, the Rumanian minister to

---

31   Incoming telegram from Ankara to secretary of state, Washington: For WRB from Hirschmann, 11 July 1944, Papers of the War Refugee Board.

32   Ibid.

33   Eric Jabotinsky, *Report on the Circumstances of the Sinking of the Turkish Motorboat MEFKURE*, 18 August 1944, Papers of the War Refugee Board.

34   William O'Dwyer, *Final Summary Report of the Executive Director, War Refugee Board*, 15 September 1945, Papers of the War Refugee Board.

Ankara, in an attempt to aid Jews who lived in the Transnistria concentration camp. In 1941 the camp was in German territory, but by early 1944 the area was nearly destroyed by clashes between the Germans and Soviets. Left in the unsanitary conditions of the camp, thousands of inmates died of disease. Despite the death toll, the WRB learned that about 48,000 Jews remained alive in Transnistria.[35] In addition to disease, the inmates faced another danger—their camp was directly in the path of the retreating German armies, which might take out their losses on the Jews. Time was running out for the Transnistria Jews, unless someone could convince the Rumanians to close the camp.

Gilbert Simond, a member of the Red Cross in Ankara, arranged a meeting between Hirschmann and Cretzianu. The Rumanian minister seemed surprised that a representative from the United States wanted to save Jews, yet Cretzianu was also intrigued by Hirschmann's offer. Hirschmann promised United States visas for Cretzianu and his family in exchange for the closure of the camp, as well as the good will of the United States toward Rumania after the war.[36] The following day, as Hirschmann sat in Ambassador Steinhardt's office, Simond called with a report from the Red Cross Representative in Bucharest. The report read, "Due to reasons unknown to me, the camp in Transnistria has been disbanded."[37] As mentioned earlier, Rumanian Jews encountered transportation difficulties when they tried to leave Rumania for Palestine via Turkey, but at least the 48,000 people from Transnistria were safeguarded from the German army and freed from the unsanitary conditions of the camp.

In the summer of 1944, Hirschmann met again with Cretzianu in an effort to save a different group of Jews. This time Hirschmann sought to create a safe haven in Rumania for Jews fleeing Hungary. Just as the WRB did with Hungarian officials, Hirschmann issued veiled threats to the Rumanian minister. By this time Allied victory

35   Ibid.
36   Hirschmann, 157.
37   Ibid.

was assured, and Hirschmann warned Cretzianu "not to permit his government to 'construct a technical wall' against these refugees from Hungary at this time."[38] Impressed by the warnings issued to Hungarian officials, Cretzianu became convinced that it would be in his government's best interest to comply with the wishes of the United States. The Rumanian minister presented Hirschmann with Rumania's commitment to temporarily receive Hungarian Jews provided that the Red Cross met their basic needs during their stay.[39]

After the war, the Soviets occupied Rumania. Though many former inmates of Transnistria survived, most now lived in a communist country. Yet some of the survivors somehow escaped to the United States, Palestine, or Canada. During a postwar speaking tour, Hirschmann met a former camp inmate who left Transnistria as a boy and escaped to Palestine. The man became a manager of a hotel in Jerusalem.[40] Hirschmann also followed through on his promise to Minister Cretzianu. Although the Russians killed other Rumanian government officials, Cretzianu and his family safely arrived in the United States.[41]

While working for the WRB, Hirschmann also took advantage of the opportunity to meet with the Bulgarian minister to Turkey, Nicholas Balabanoff, in early 1944. The Bulgarian leadership at the time was unreceptive to Hirschmann's suggestion that Bulgarians aid Jews living in their country, but Hirschmann tried a different tactic when the leadership changed hands. This time he gave Balabanoff specific demands to take back to his government. The United States, Hirschmann told him, wanted Bulgaria to permit Jews to travel by rail from Bulgaria to Turkey.[42] From there, refugees would move on to Palestine.

Hirschmann also made another request of the Bulgarian

---

38 Telegram from Hirschmann, Ankara for Pehle WRB, 7 August 1944, Papers of the War Refugee Board.
39 Ibid.
40 Hirschmann, 159–60.
41 Ibid., 160.
42 Memorandum by Ira Hirschmann, 13 July 1944, Papers of the War Refugee Board.

minister. For some time, Bulgarian Jews had lived under oppressive laws that denied them the same rights as other Bulgarians. When Bulgaria joined the Axis powers in 1941, Jews struggled to find work or even to hold on to their homes. Norbert J. Yasharoff's family was already confined to the second floor of their home, but they were forced to give up that space also. Yasharoff explained that another couple wanted to move into the house that had ties to the fascist authorities. As a result, his family was "given the order to vacate in less than a week. We moved downstairs into the apartment that was used before as an office ... [T]hey—the Bulgarian lawyer and his German wife—moved in. They conducted a sort of cleansing with holy water and everything ... to cleanse the Jewish spirit out of the apartment."[43] By 1944, however, the Axis powers were clearly losing the war, and Hirschmann insisted that the Bulgarian government repeal its oppressive Jewish laws. In return, he promised that the United States government would remember the goodwill of the Bulgarian authorities toward Jews when the war ended.

The promise of postwar goodwill from the United States made a favorable impression on the Bulgarian officials. In July Balabanoff told Hirschmann that Bulgaria had every intention of changing its policies toward the Jews; however, he indicated that changes would take place gradually.[44] In August, with the anti-Jewish laws in Bulgaria still on the books, Hirschmann arranged for another meeting with Balabanoff at Gilbert Simond's home. In his account of the meeting, Hirschmann mentioned that Balabanoff arrived late and took some of Hirschmann's cigarettes. He stated, "I took no steps against this overt act since I determined to take measures to make him pay for them [the cigarettes] in large proportions."[45] Hirschmann felt Balabanoff could pay him back by pressuring his government to

---

43   Norbert J. Yasharoff, interview by United States Holocaust Museum, 1989, transcript United States Holocaust Museum Oral History Collection, Washington, DC.

44   Incoming telegram from Hirschmann, Ankara for Pehle WRB, 26 July 1944, Papers of the War Refugee Board.

45   Memorandum for Mr. Kelley, conversation with Mr. Balabanoff Bulgarian Minister to Turkey, 5 August 1944, Papers of the War Refugee Board.

withdraw the anti-Jewish laws immediately. Hirschmann "asserted that nothing short of the abrogation of these two laws would satisfy us … and that it was up to the Bulgarian government with one stroke at this time to disassociate itself with this black chapter in its history; otherwise it remains as direct evidence of association with the Nazis."[46] By making this statement, Hirschmann gave the Bulgarian government two choices: it could either eliminate its anti-Semitic laws and gain the approval of the United States, or face the consequences of America's postwar disapproval. After Hirschmann's speech, Balabanoff promised that evening to send a strong message to his government regarding the repeal of the laws.[47]

Unlike his conversations with the Rumanian minister, Hirschmann's negotiations with Balabanoff focused on the repeal of anti-Jewish laws rather than Jewish immigration. His approach had advantages for both the Bulgarian economy and for the Jews living in Bulgaria. Hirschmann pointed out to Balabanoff that the Bulgarian minister of commerce "declared that the elimination of Jews from the economic life of the country was to a large extent responsible for the 'catastrophic' position of [the] Bulgarian economy."[48] If the Bulgarian government allowed Jews to earn a living again, they could help rebuild postwar Bulgaria. The arrangement also gave the Jews the advantage of staying in their homeland rather than relocating, since there would likely be difficulty in finding a haven for them as there had been with the other Jews the WRB attempted to relocate. Instead of moving the Jews, Hirschmann proposed that the War Refugee Board and other relief agencies provide basic necessities to Bulgarian Jews until they had the opportunity to earn their own money.[49]

By mid-August the Bulgarian government showed signs of relenting to Hirschmann's demands to eliminate the oppressive Jewish laws. Hirschmann received a letter from the president of the Istanbul

46   Ibid.
47   Ibid.
48   Ibid.
49   Letter from Hirschmann to Mr. Simond, 8 August 1944, Papers of the War Refugee Board.

American College, which indicated that Bulgaria's political climate had changed for the better.[50] The letter proved to be prophetic—by the end of August Bulgaria's anti-Jewish laws were repealed.

---

50   Letter from Floyd H. Black, President of Istanbul American College to Ira
        Hirschmann, American Embassy Istanbul, 15 August 1944, Papers of the War
        Refugee Board.

CHAPTER EIGHT

The WRB in Sweden: The Accomplishments of Field Representative Iver Olsen

DESPITE IRA HIRSCHMANN'S SUCCESSES IN Turkey, John Pehle realized the necessity of having more than one War Refugee Board representative in neutral territory. Iver Olsen, the Treasury's representative in Stockholm, Sweden, received a request to represent the Board in March of 1944. Like Hirschmann, Olsen received instructions to implement the Board's policies regarding rescue and relief of refugees who managed to reach the neutral country in which he worked.[1] Both he and the Board hoped to capitalize on his connections with Swedish government officials to bring Jews out of neighboring Axis nations and into Sweden.

One country that Olsen worked to bring Jews out of was practically next door to Sweden. Unlike neutral Sweden, Finland was allied with the Axis powers. Though no mass deportations from Finland had occurred yet, Olsen and the WRB decided that as many Finnish Jews as possible should be moved into Sweden in case the Nazis changed their minds. Olsen knew that if the Germans decided to expand the war zone in Finland, more Jews would be in danger. Herschel Johnson, America's minister to Stockholm and an important partner in Olsen's rescue efforts, noted the Finnish government's willingness to allow emigration of Jews who feared what the Nazis might do in the future. By July 1944 the Finns

---

1   Telegram to Minister Johnson, American Legation in Stockholm from secretary of state in Washington, DC, 28 March 1944, Papers of the War Refugee Board.

provided verbal assurances that Jews who wanted to leave for Sweden could do so.[2]

At first the possibility of Finnish Jews arriving in Sweden seemed hopeful. The Finns provided exit visas and the Swedes provided entry visas for fifty-seven Jewish refugees. But another group of sixty-two Jews were refused entry visas by the Swedes.[3] In contrast to the enthusiasm of the Finns who demonstrated their willingness to help Jews leave their country, the Jewish communities in Stockholm showed little interest in helping Jews to enter Sweden. Olsen reported that the Jews in Stockholm were "strangely apathetic" toward his efforts to bring stateless Jews into Sweden.[4] Perhaps Swedish Jews, like some in America, feared that an influx of Jewish immigrants would increase anti-Semitism in their country. Regardless of their reasons, the indifference of Sweden's Jews caused some potential immigrants who might otherwise have left Finland to stay. Fortunately the Jews in Finland were not exterminated; however, Olsen had no way of guaranteeing their safety at the time. Like other dedicated WRB representatives, Olsen took every precaution to save Jews.

While Jewish immigration to Sweden from Finland was limited, Olsen and Johnson convinced the Swedes to take in a small number of refugees. By July 11, 1944, Johnson reported to the Board that "evacuation of stateless Jews is proceeding by regular sailings and in a week or so approximately fifty will probably have arrived in Sweden."[5] Of course, the Swedish people did not offer to help the refugees with food and clothes once they arrived in Sweden. With a combination of American Jewish Joint Distribution Committee and WRB funds, however, the refugees received provisions. In all,

---

2   Telegram to secretary of state in Washington, DC, from Johnson, American Legation in Stockholm, 6 July 1944, Papers of the War Refugee Board.

3   Telegram to secretary of state in Washington, DC, from Johnson, American Legation in Stockholm, 3 July 1944, Papers of the War Refugee Board.

4   Telegram to secretary of state in Washington, DC, from Johnson, American Legation in Stockholm, 6 July 1944, Papers of the War Refugee Board.

5   Telegram to secretary of state in Washington, DC, from Johnson, American Legation in Stockholm, 11 July 1944, Papers of the War Refugee Board.

about 150 Finnish Jews arrived in Sweden.[6] Many others never came, but even this small number was an accomplishment given the obstacles Olsen faced in bringing any Jewish refugees to Sweden.

In addition to his attempts to bring Jews out of Finland, Olsen also tried to rescue Jews and political refugees in Estonia, Latvia, and Lithuania. He helped organize teams of people to carry out rescues directly in each of these countries. With WRB funds Olsen obtained fast-cabin cruisers, fuel, supplies, and false IDs to bring potential refugees to Sweden.[7] Again, his efforts encountered considerable obstacles. One obstacle was timing. The War Refugee Board was created in 1944, which meant that fewer Jews remained alive in the Baltic States.[8] In addition the rescue teams only got going in the summer. The long periods of daylight made it more difficult to smuggle refugees in under the cover of darkness.[9] The Lithuanian and Latvian rescue teams faced additional obstacles. Lithuanian rescue efforts suffered because the head of the team's operations and its best source of intelligence disappeared.[10] Without its knowledgeable leader, the Lithuanian team had little hope of saving many lives. Olsen's Latvian operation stalled for yet another reason. The small number of Latvians in Sweden made it difficult to put together a rescue team at all.[11] Nevertheless, Olsen determined to do the best job possible under difficult circumstances. The rescue team in Estonia was the most successful. By August 1944 several hundred Estonian refugees were on their way to Sweden. The refugees were intellectuals "much wanted by the Germans" but included no Jews.[12] Olsen hoped that the Latvian and Lithuanian operations would bring out some refugees

---

6   *Report on the Operations of the WRB from Stockholm, Sweden*, 20 November 1944, Papers of the War Refugee Board.

7   Wyman, *The Abandonment*, 229.

8   Ibid.

9   Letter to the WRB from Iver Olsen, WRB Representative in Stockholm, Sweden, 20 November 1944, Papers of the War Refugee Board.

10 Ibid.

11 Ibid.

12 Ibid.

but did not expect significant results. By the time rescue efforts were called off in September, the Baltic rescue teams had saved more than 1,200 political refugees.[13] Although the saving of any human lives was an amazing feat under the circumstances, Olsen's rescue teams failed to rescue any Jews.

The WRB's representative in Sweden did more than organize rescues for potential immigrants. Both Olsen and Johnson continued to work on behalf of the new political and Jewish immigrants after their arrival in Sweden. Johnson sent a letter to the secretary of state in which he reported the creation of two Swedish hospitals and a soup kitchen for refugees.[14] Although only a small number of immigrants came to Sweden, the WRB's representative tried his best to aid those who arrived in his assigned country.

Olsen's greatest success in terms of numbers of people rescued came from the 1945 rescue operations in Norway. The American Labor and Relief for Norway financed the rescue and relief program that brought Norwegians to Sweden. In all, about 15,000 Norwegians described as being "in serious jeopardy" escaped to Sweden.[15] All of these people somehow ran afoul of the Nazis, which endangered their lives. Olsen did not encounter resistance from the Swedish authorities during these efforts. In fact, the program went forward smoothly thanks in large part to the cooperation of the Swedes. In addition to rescue, Sweden helped organize relief efforts for suffering Norwegians. For example, the Norwegian Church in Sweden helped smuggle food and clothes into Norway.[16] The sudden helpfulness of the Swedes may have been due to the fact that none of the Norwegian refugees were Jewish.

---

13   Wyman, *The Abandonment*, 229.

14   Telegram to the secretary of state in Washington, DC, from Johnson in Stockholm, 22 December 1944, Papers of the War Refugee Board.

15   *Final Report of the Activities of War Refugee Board from Sweden*, 15 June 1945, Papers of the War Refugee Board.

16   Ibid.

The War Refugee Board's operations in Sweden accomplished little for the Jews, but Olsen and Johnson made one final push to safeguard Jews near the end of the war. Olsen secretly met with various German contacts in Sweden. He expressed the revulsion of the United States toward maltreatment of the Jews and other prisoners of war to three different contacts. By March 1945 Olsen's discussion with one of these contacts, Dr. Fritz Hesse, seemed to be making some headway. Olsen believed that Hesse made contact with him because the Germans wanted to send out peace feelers and procure the good will of the United States.[17] In particular Hesse was interested in discussing the fate of German POWs. Olsen's next contact was Dr. Kleist, who had connections to high-ranking Nazi officials. Like Hesse, Kleist assured Olsen that "no further steps would be taken to destroy the Jews and other civilian prisoners."[18] Based on these discussions and others, a meeting was set up between a member of Stockholm's Jewish community and Nazi leader Heinrich Himmler on April 19 in Berlin. The meeting resulted in the release of several thousand Jews from the Ravensbruck concentration camp.[19]

The arrival of thousands of refugees in the spring of 1945 represented one of Olsen's greatest achievements as the WRB's representative in Sweden. Most of the 7,000 refugees who arrived in Sweden were women from the Ravensbruck camp, though a small number of men came from other concentration camps. Half of the Ravensbruck group were Jewish refugees.[20] American Minister Johnson monitored the condition of the refugees. Many required medical attention due to malnutrition, while others suffered from exhaustion. When the refugees explained the conditions they had endured in the camps, their survival seemed miraculous. Female refugees reported working twelve-hour days, which consisted of

---

17   Ibid.
18   Ibid.
19   Ibid.
20   Wyman, *The Abandonment*, 231.

physical labor, such as digging ditches.[21] To fuel their work, the refugees received only soup and coffee with the occasional piece of bread. Johnson found it disturbing that only the "healthy" inmates were permitted to leave Ravensbruck for Sweden as most refugees arrived at half their normal weight.[22] Nothing could be done for the refugees whom the Nazis refused to send to Sweden. Nevertheless, those who came received aid from both the WRB and the Swedes.

Although Olsen complained about the apathy of Swedes toward Jewish refugees, exceptions existed. Hundreds of volunteers from the Swedish city of Malmo aided doctors and nurses who attended to the Ravensbruck refugees. Many of these refugees were housed in schools because of overcrowding in the hospitals.[23] Much-needed food, clothing, and supplies arrived from different parts of the country. The helpfulness of the local community allowed the refugees to thrive. However, these men and women would have remained in camps if not for Olsen's secret negotiations.

After he left Sweden, Olsen received much criticism for his failure to save large numbers of Jews. Yet as already noted, he worked under unfavorable conditions for large-scale rescue operations. The reluctance of the local Jewish community to welcome refugees, the small number of Jews remaining in the Balkans, and even the timing of potential rescue efforts prevented Olsen from accomplishing many of his goals. Olsen never regretted taking the WRB post in Sweden, though he did regret his inability to do more for Jews. He wrote in a letter to the WRB, "It seems to me that I must have run down a thousand or so straw possibilities in trying to obtain concrete results [to rescue Jews] and wish that more of them could have panned out."[24] Despite his own frustrations, anyone who witnessed Olsen's efforts agreed that he did his best under difficult

---

21   Telegram to secretary of state, Washington, DC, from Johnson in Stockholm, 3 May 1945, Papers of the War Refugee Board.

22   Ibid.

23   Ibid.

24   Letter to WRB from Iver Olsen, WRB Representative in Stockholm, 10 August 1944, Papers of the War Refugee Board.

circumstances. In autumn of 1944, a member of the American Jewish Joint Distribution Committee visited Sweden. Her report to the JDC expressed her conviction that Olsen did everything possible in order to save Jewish lives.[25]

25   Report from Laura Margolis, JDC Representative, November 1944, Papers of the War Refugee Board.

CHAPTER NINE

The WRB in Switzerland: The Accomplishments of Field Representative Roswell McClelland

IN MARCH OF 1944, THE Board chose thirty-year-old Roswell McClelland to run its rescue operations in Switzerland. Despite his young age, McClelland already knew much about refugee relief work. Both he and his wife had worked previously for the American Friends Service Committee in France. His earlier work had given McClelland not only experience with the needs of refugees but also knowledge of how the Nazis thought and acted.[1] McClelland's work on behalf of the Board extended to several countries where Jews needed aid, including Italy, France, Hungary, and Rumania.

Through McClelland, the Board rendered limited but valuable assistance to Jews in Northern Italy. After his appointment to the WRB in spring of 1944, McClelland received requests from Italian Jewish leaders who asked for permission to enter Switzerland as refugees. They also asked for protection and financial aid for Jews unable to leave Italy. McClelland felt that the only reasonable thing he could do for Jews in Northern Italy was to ensure that they had funds for food and clothing by contacting Saly Mayer, the representative of the American Jewish Joint Distribution Committee. Through Mayer, McClelland received a guarantee that more than $120,000 would be sent to Jewish organizations in Rome.[2] Later

---

1   Morse, 330.
2   Letter to Harold Tittmann, Esquire, American charge d'affaires, Vatican City from Roswell McClelland, 24 May 1944; Folder: Jews in German Occupied Italy; General Correspondence of R. McClelland; Papers of the War Refugee Board; Franklin D. Roosevelt Library, Hyde Park, NY.

that summer McClelland learned that the JDC's funds provided aid for Jews in several regions of the country.[3]

Other than sending money, however, McClelland made few promises to the Jewish community in Italy. Legal emigration could not take place because Italy was occupied by Germany. Italy's borders were well guarded by the SS, which made even clandestine escape difficult. McClelland stated that although the Swiss would likely receive refugees from Rome, the difficulty lay in trying to bring them safely out of Italy.[4] Though doubtful of success, McClelland responded to the efforts of the Italian Resistance movement to smuggle Jews out of the country in summer 1944. During that period many Jews were rounded up, arrested, and finally deported when the camps they were in filled up. McClelland's source of information was Gerhart Riegner, who had proven his credibility with regard to the plight of Jews in Europe prior to the Board's creation. Riegner endorsed the Italian underground's efforts to help Jews escape or hide from their pursuers.

Though he harbored doubts about the results that could be achieved by the Resistance movement, Riegner's endorsement led McClelland to request the WRB to express its approval of Italian rescue operations.[5] The Board granted his request, authorizing McClelland to support such rescue projects and provide financial aid at his discretion.[6] For example, the Board made major financial contributions to the work of the Women's Defense Groups, which

---

3   Telegram to WRB from McClelland, paraphrase of Riegner to JDC, 4 July 1944; Folder: Jews in German Occupied Italy; General Correspondence of R. McClelland; Papers of the War Refugee Board; Franklin D. Roosevelt Library, Hyde Park, NY.

4   Letter to Harold Tittmann, Esquire, American charge d'affaires, Vatican City from Roswell McClelland, 24 May 1944; Folder: Jews in German Occupied Italy; General Correspondence of R. McClelland; Papers of the War Refugee Board; Franklin D. Roosevelt Library, Hyde Park, NY.

5   Telegram to WRB from McClelland, 7 August 1944; Folder: Jews in German Occupied Italy; General Correspondence of R. McClelland; Papers of the War Refugee Board; Franklin D. Roosevelt Library, Hyde Park, NY.

6   Telegram to McClelland from WRB, 29 August 1944; Folder: Jews in German Occupied Italy; General Correspondence of R. McClelland; Papers of the War Refugee Board; Franklin D. Roosevelt Library, Hyde Park, NY.

helped support families of those who were imprisoned or killed by the enemy. The Defense Groups either provided places for these families to hide or transferred them to safer locations. Despite the obstacles involved, the Women's Defense Groups managed to smuggle ten families into Switzerland during the late summer of 1944 and early spring of 1945.[7] Some of the WRB's aid also directly impacted those threatened with deportation or death. WRB funds helped finance prison breaks through the summer of 1944, which resulted in the escape of about thirty-five people.[8]

McClelland heard about an opportunity to support a unique rescue project in October 1944. The proposed plan involved psychological warfare techniques against Italian authorities that would hopefully bring refugees out of Italian internment camps. The papal nuncio in Italy agreed to send a message to the fascist Minister of the Interior Buffarini to be delivered by Bruno Kiniger, the former fascist representative in Switzerland. The message explained that it was in Buffarini's interest to "find a means of releasing all internees whose lives are threatened by deportation and/or massacre by the Axis."[9] Since Hitler was taking less personal interest in the fascist camps at this point in the war, Kiniger offered to write his own letter to Buffarini. Kiniger's "strongly worded letter" stated that Buffarini's failure to act on behalf of the internees would label him as a war criminal.[10] Both letters suggested that Buffarini hand over the internees, most of whom were Jewish, to Switzerland. One problem with the plan outlined in the letters was the tight control the fascist

7   *Report on the Activities of the WRB Through its Representation at the American Legation in Bern, Switzerland, March 1944–July 1945*; Folder: Programs with Respect to Relief and Rescue of Refugees: Evacuations to and through Switzerland; General Correspondence of R. McClelland; Papers of the War Refugee Board; Franklin D. Roosevelt Library, Hyde Park, NY.

8   Ibid.

9   Memo on the North Italy Project to Howard Wriggins, Intergovernmental Committee on Refugees from Sir Clifford Heathcote-Smith, 27 October 1944; Folder: Jews in German Occupied Italy; General Correspondence of R. McClelland; Papers of the War Refugee Board; Franklin D. Roosevelt Library, Hyde Park, NY.

10 Ibid.

German troops held near the Italian border, which made it difficult for anyone to leave. Another difficulty lay in Switzerland's lack of recognition of the Italian fascist government. Poor relations between the two governments limited Switzerland's ability to put diplomatic pressure on Italy. Nevertheless, both the British representative from the Intergovernmental Committee on Refugees (ICR), Clifford Heathcote-Smith, and McClelland agreed that the messages should be sent, so Kiniger went to Milan to deliver them. McClelland also proposed meeting with Buffarini personally in order to put even more pressure on the minister.[11] Even if the internees could not be rescued, McClelland hoped to at least gain better treatment for them in the camps.

Neither man knew if the plan would rescue any Jews, but the ICR representative expressed his confidence in McClelland. After he learned of Kiniger's departure, Heathcote-Smith wrote, "I was delighted to receive ... the gist of your telegram, to the effect that the machinery regarding internees in North Italy had now been set in motion. Well done ... As a precedent for other possible similar methods of release, and still more for the sake of the individuals concerned whose lives may be thus saved, I would urge you—if I thought it were necessary to do so—to plug away for all you are worth at this project."[12] As Heathcote-Smith knew, McClelland required no prodding when the possibility of saving human lives existed. Yet there was little McClelland could do at that moment except endorse the proposal and hope for positive results. Regrettably McClelland learned in spring 1945 that although Buffarini received the letter from Kiniger, the plan to rescue internees had never materialized.[13]

---

11   Ibid.

12   Letter to R. McClelland from Clifford Heathcote-Smith, Intergovernmental
     Committee on Refugees, 27 October 1944; Folder: Jews in German Occupied
     Italy; General Correspondence of R. McClelland; Papers of the War Refugee
     Board; Franklin D. Roosevelt Library, Hyde Park, NY.

13   Telegram to Heathcote-Smith of Intergovernmental Committee from McClelland,
     6 April 1945; Folder: Jews in German Occupied Italy; General Correspondence
     of R. McClelland; Papers of the War Refugee Board; Franklin D. Roosevelt Library,
     Hyde Park, NY.

Yet the mission yielded some positive results. Thanks to Kiniger's intervention, Buffarini agreed to allow limited food and medical relief to detainees in the San Vittore prison in Milan.[14]

Throughout 1945 McClelland continued the most successful means of helping Jews in Northern Italy—providing WRB funds to groups working to aid those persecuted by the Nazis. For example, McClelland gave 6,000 Swiss francs to a church-sponsored group that provided protection for Jewish refugees.[15] McClelland made clear that such funds could only be used to help people who were involved in protecting and hiding refugees or the refugees themselves.

Though physical rescue proved difficult in Northern Italy because of SS and fascist patrolling of the border, the WRB and McClelland pursued every possible method of aid. In McClelland's opinion, every life was worth saving, even if WRB funds could help only a limited number of people. Overall, WRB aid in Northern Italy was limited to providing funds to Resistance groups for the maintenance of persecuted people. Nevertheless, those funds undoubtedly saved many people from starvation and exposure in the camps, as well as providing protection to workers attempting to help them.

The War Refugee Board and McClelland had more success when providing aid to French refugees. Switzerland and France had existing social and economic ties on which a relationship between rescue organizations on both sides could be built. For example, many French Resistance groups had unofficial representatives based in Switzerland, a fact that gave McClelland easy access to information

---

14   *Report on the Activities of the WRB through its Representation at the American Legation in Bern, Switzerland, March 1944–July 1945*; Folder: Programs with Respect to Relief and Rescue of Refugees: Evacuations to and through Switzerland; General Correspondence of R. McClelland; Papers of the War Refugee Board; Franklin D. Roosevelt Library, Hyde Park, NY.

15   Letter to Pastor Rivoir from McClelland, 14 April 1945; Folder: Jews in German Occupied Italy; General Correspondence of R. McClelland; Papers of the War Refugee Board; Franklin D. Roosevelt Library, Hyde Park, NY.

about refugees.[16] McClelland followed up on this information with ideas for WRB rescue and relief.

French Resistance groups as well as the Board took an active interest in the safety of French children who faced deportation. The French union Oeuvre de Secours aux Enfants (OSE) successfully falsified the identity of nearly 5,000 children and placed the children with non-Jewish families.[17] Since the American Jewish Joint Distribution Committee and other Jewish organizations provided funding for the OSE, the WRB decided to use its authority to help with rescue efforts for children.

Though the Swiss had a fairly liberal policy for admitting children from France, the United States wanted Switzerland to take more adult refugees. Like the State Department in 1943, the Swiss worried that Jewish adults would become a burden on their economy. The United States hoped to circumvent this concern by providing 4,000 United States immigration visas to refugee children in Switzerland. According to McClelland, the WRB and the State Department were "motivated by the belief that assurance that a certain block of refugee children would not remain here after the war would encourage the Swiss to admit additional adult refugees."[18] The WRB also stated its willingness to pay any expenses for the young refugees while they lived in Switzerland.[19]

---

16   *Report on the Activities of the WRB through its Representation at the American Legation in Bern, Switzerland, March 1944–July 1945*; Folder: Programs with Respect to Relief and Rescue of Refugees: Evacuations to and through Switzerland; General Correspondence of R. McClelland; Papers of the War Refugee Board; Franklin D. Roosevelt Library, Hyde Park, NY.

17   Ibid.

18   Telegram to WRB from McClelland, 6 July 1944; Folder: US Immigration Visas for Refugee Children in Switzerland, March–August, November, and December 1944; General Correspondence of R. McClelland; Papers of the War Refugee Board; Franklin D. Roosevelt Library, Hyde Park, NY.

19   Telegram to Consulate in Switzerland from Hull at State Department, 18 March 1944; Folder: US Immigration Visas for Refugee Children in Switzerland, March–August, November, and December 1944; General Correspondence of R. McClelland; Papers of the War Refugee Board; Franklin D. Roosevelt Library, Hyde Park, NY.

As always, plans to bring refugees of any age into Switzerland proved challenging. French children who attempted to emigrate faced some special obstacles. These included the rough terrain between France and Switzerland, which allowed only the strongest refugees to escape. Instability in certain areas following the Normandy invasions also created problems, as did a disruption of transportation in France. On July 15, American Minister to Switzerland Leland Harrison estimated that the number of children requesting immigration visas to the United States would not exceed 500.[20] This number was a far cry from the number of visas that the State Department issued, but at least the WRB and the United States government had some success in bringing children out of France via Switzerland. McClelland's final report showed that about 600 abandoned children were brought into Switzerland and another 600 entered with their parents.[21] Unlike the efforts in Northern Italy that focused mainly on providing aid to refugees who could not leave, in France the WRB could claim a significant achievement in getting refugees out of the country.

McClelland's hope that Switzerland would admit more adult refugees remained unrealized. He made an unofficial arrangement with the Swiss police to get advance consent for the entry of the most endangered individuals in France.[22] Nevertheless, incidents occurred in which refugees who came to Switzerland were turned back. Some Swiss border police made snap judgments about refugees and assumed that they were trying to enter illegally. In order to prevent such mishaps, McClelland handed out bribes to

---

20   Telegram to State Department from Harrison, 15 July 1944; Folder: US Immigration
      Visas for Refugee Children in Switzerland, March–August, November, and
      December 1944; General Correspondence of R. McClelland; Papers of the War
      Refugee Board; Franklin D. Roosevelt Library, Hyde Park, NY.

21   *Report on the Activities of the WRB through its Representation at the American Legation in
      Bern, Switzerland, March 1944–July 1945*; Folder: Programs with Respect to Relief
      and Rescue of Refugees: Evacuations to and through Switzerland; General
      Correspondence of R. McClelland; Papers of the War Refugee Board; Franklin D.
      Roosevelt Library, Hyde Park, NY.

22   Ibid.

Swiss officials responsible for screening refugees. In return, the officials kept refugees whom the police suspected in a safe place until McClelland's office could investigate each case.[23] Overall, Switzerland took in more refugees than any of its European counterparts even though the Swiss sometimes resisted an influx of refugees.

Unlike the direct rescue efforts of the WRB, sometimes opportunities to rescue Jews grew out of WRB relief efforts. For example, WRB funds aided Spaniards and Germans who languished in internment camps as well as those who hid from the authorities either because they were Jews or because of their political connections. McClelland sent grants to the Spanish for two reasons. First, the money went to help the Spanish organize aid for their countrymen and women. Secondly, the funds were used to pay for special Spanish guides who agreed to assist in rescue efforts. These guides enabled small groups of Jewish refugees to pass from the Pyrenees into Spain.[24] In return, the guides received small goods that were difficult to find during the war, such as pocketknives, soap, cigarettes, and Swiss watches.[25] Like the overland route from France to Switzerland, the route through the Pyrenees presented a challenge to all but the strongest refugees. A hike through the mountains took ten to fourteen hours.[26] Despite the hardships of the journey, McClelland estimated that between 700 and 1,000 people escaped with the help of their Spanish guides.[27] McClelland's contacts and experience in refugee work played an important part

---

23 Ibid.

24 Letter to Donald Lowrie of Young Men's Christian Association from McClelland, 7 July 1944; Folder: Jews in France—WRB Relief Action: April–October 1944; General Correspondence of R. McClelland; Papers of the War Refugee Board; Franklin D. Roosevelt Library, Hyde Park, NY.

25 Morse, 331.

26 Ibid.

27 *Report on the Activities of the WRB through its Representation at the American Legation in Bern, Switzerland, March 1944–July 1945*; Folder: Programs with Respect to Relief and Rescue of Refugees: Evacuations to and through Switzerland; General Correspondence of R. McClelland; Papers of the War Refugee Board; Franklin D. Roosevelt Library, Hyde Park, NY.

in the success of this mission. He brought the Spanish committees in contact with the Jewish committees in Switzerland. In this way, Swiss representatives of Jewish organizations were aware of the rescue efforts of the Spaniards and sent funds to support the guides.

Though McClelland concentrated on rescue efforts for French refugees, he did not ignore opportunities to provide supplies to those unable to leave. When members of the Service Social (the French relief organization) contacted him and explained their financial problems, McClelland was sympathetic. The Service Social tried to provide supplies for political prisoners in camps and their family members, but the organization had inadequate funding. McClelland realized the importance of the Service Social's work. In an uncharacteristic move, he decided to grant WRB money to the Service Social before he contacted Washington. Only later did he send a letter to the WRB explaining his contribution of 200,000 Swiss francs to the relief organization's budget.[28] Technically, WRB representatives like McClelland did not have the authority to help people who were not, as the president stated in his executive order, in imminent danger of death.[29] Yet the Board agreed with McClelland's actions. In response to his request to continue funding the Service Social, the Board sent McClelland a telegram authorizing him to "continue such support as long as you may judge it to be advisable."[30] Both the WRB's director and his subordinates understood the need to occasionally step outside the bounds of the executive order so that more lives could be saved.

The WRB's rescue efforts in Hungary involved a combination of political pressure and funding of rescue projects. In May 1944 the world learned of the deportation of Hungarian Jews. McClelland

---

28   Telegram to WRB from McClelland, 31 July 1944; Folder: Jews in France—WRB
      Relief Action: April–October 1944; General Correspondence of R. McClelland;
      Papers of the War Refugee Board; Franklin D. Roosevelt Library, Hyde Park, NY.
29   Franklin D. Roosevelt, Executive Order No. 9417, 22 January 1944, Papers of the
      War Refugee Board.
30   Telegram from WRB to McClelland, 23 August 1944; Folder: Jews in France—WRB
      Relief Action: April–October 1944; General Correspondence of R. McClelland;
      Papers of the War Refugee Board; Franklin D. Roosevelt Library, Hyde Park, NY.

helped the Swiss to send messages to Hungary that expressed the Swiss and American governments' disapproval of the deportations. The messages reminded the Hungarians that the United States was determined "to see to it that all those who share the guilt (of such acts) shall share the punishment."[31] The Hungarians were not the only ones who needed to be convinced to help the Jews, however. As seen in the case of French refugees, some people in Switzerland showed their willingness to help Jews, while others resisted. Through McClelland, the Swiss government received frequent reminders of the concern the United States government had for the Jews, at least when the United States found a neutral country to drop them in without having to increase its immigration quotas. Although the American government's words contradicted its actions, McClelland was able to secure some concessions for refugees from the Swiss. In Budapest, Hungary, the Swiss mission issued protective documents to holders of Palestine certificates and sought to protect from deportation the holders of Latin American documents. While under pressure from the United States, Switzerland decided to send its own warning to the Hungarian government. The Swiss minister in Budapest received instructions "to leave no doubt in the mind of the Hungarian government with regard to the attitude of the Swiss government and the Swiss people concerning these persecutions and to make it clear ... that the good relations and the high regard which the Swiss government and people had for Hungary would undoubtedly be adversely effected [sic] by a continuance of this policy."[32] The effect of the Swiss government's psychological warfare techniques on Hungarian officials cannot be quantified. However, as seen in Chapter Five, Admiral Horthy decided in the summer of 1944 to stop deportations of the Jews. Pressure from a country like

---

31   *Report on the Activities of the WRB through its Representation at the American Legation in Bern, Switzerland, March 1944–July 1945*; Folder: Programs with Respect to Relief and Rescue of Refugees: Evacuations to and through Switzerland; General Correspondence of R. McClelland; Papers of the War Refugee Board; Franklin D. Roosevelt Library, Hyde Park, NY.

32   Ibid.

Switzerland, which Hungary historically had better relations with than the United States, could only help save the lives of Hungarian Jews.

Underground groups who received financial aid from the WRB plotted the escape of Hungarian Jews. One Zionist rescue group, called the Hechaluz, focused on getting Jews out of Hungary and into the safer zones of Rumania and Yugoslavia. When the deportation of Jews from Hungary ceased for a brief time in summer 1944, Hechaluz members wisely used the respite to help Jews leave the country. McClelland contributed nearly 200,000 Swiss francs to Hechaluz in July and August 1944.[33] WRB funds paid for transportation, supplies, false papers, and bribes for low-level Rumanian and Hungarian officials who agreed to let Jews enter or leave their countries. Unlike some other rescue organizations, the Hechaluz proved very effective in helping Jews escape. Though the break in deportations made their work somewhat easier than that of other groups, the Hechaluz leadership foresaw that the cessation of deportations was temporary. The sense of urgency that members felt enabled a great deal of work to be done in a short period of time. As McClelland pointed out in a telegram to the WRB, Hechaluz made the most of the short time they had to get Jews out. By mid-July 1,650 Jews had already left for Rumania, while about 200 waited to cross the border.[34] The Hechaluz did not plan to leave refugees in Rumania if transport to Palestine was possible, however. Funds for steam transportation for Jewish refugees who could leave Rumania for Palestine came from the WRB and the American Jewish Joint Distribution Committee.[35]

Although Hechaluz had the most success getting Hungarian Jews

---

33   Telegram to WRB from McClelland, 17 August 1944, Folder: Jews in Hungary: August 1944; General Correspondence of R. McClelland; Papers of the War Refugee Board; Franklin D. Roosevelt Library, Hyde Park, NY.

34   Ibid.

35   *Report on the Activities of the WRB through its Representation at the American Legation in Bern, Switzerland, March 1944–July 1945*; Folder: Programs with Respect to Relief and Rescue of Refugees: Evacuations to and through Switzerland; General Correspondence of R. McClelland; Papers of the War Refugee Board; Franklin D. Roosevelt Library, Hyde Park, NY.

into Rumania, they explored other possible havens. For example, a few hundred Hungarian Jews reached Yugoslavia thanks to the efforts of Hechaluz and the funds the group received from McClelland.[36]

Another rescue success story came from the negotiations between Swiss citizen Saly Mayer and Nazi officials (discussed in Chapter Five). Mayer's talent for stringing the Nazis along resulted in the entry of over 1,000 Jews from concentration camps into Switzerland. Swiss hospitality for the former camp inmates did not last long, though. The refugees wanted to stay in Switzerland until they could either return to Hungary or leave for Palestine, but the Swiss government refused their requests. In fact the Swiss government made it clear "that each refugee leaving will be a relief to the country."[37] Refugees who reached Switzerland after surviving concentration camps had to move again, this time to camps in North Africa. A large group of over 1,000 refugees prepared to leave in railroad cars.[38] Though the travel conditions were more sanitary than those provided by the Nazis and the destination was not a death camp, the refugees must have felt the irony of again leaving by train for an internment camp. A group of Bergen-Belsen refugees wrote to McClelland, expressing their gratitude for his efforts to rescue them from "the Bergen-Belsen hell," but also with the "hope that liberty would not remain the monopoly of only those who possessed it up to the present."[39] On occasion the Swiss government changed its policy and allowed refugees to stay. For example, in July 1945 McClelland

---

36   Wyman, *The Abandonment*, 233.
37   Telegram to Sir Herbert Emerson from Intergovernmental Committee Representative Heinrich Rothmund, 20 April 1945; Folder: Jews in Hungary and Bergen-Belsen Group: Jan.–June 1945; General Correspondence of R. McClelland; Papers of the War Refugee Board; Franklin D. Roosevelt Library, Hyde Park, NY.
38   Telegram to WRB from McClelland, 19 April 1945; Folder: Jews in Hungary and Bergen-Belsen Group: Jan.–June 1945; General Correspondence of R. McClelland; Papers of the War Refugee Board; Franklin D. Roosevelt Library, Hyde Park, NY.
39   Letter to Roswell McClelland from refugee camp, 24 April 1945; Folder: Jews in Hungary and Bergen-Belsen Group: Jan.–June 1945; General Correspondence of R. McClelland; Papers of the War Refugee Board; Franklin D. Roosevelt Library, Hyde Park, NY.

sent a telegram to the American Embassy in Rome, stating that the Swiss authorities had decided not to insist on evacuating a group of 750 Jews because the United States guaranteed their maintenance.[40] Another 706 Jews headed for Palestine, however, were evacuated from Switzerland by train and needed accommodations in Italy for about two weeks before they reached Palestine.[41] Though the WRB did its utmost to care for refugees during their temporary stay in Switzerland, it did not always overcome the impatience of the Swiss to get refugees out sooner rather than later.

As seen in previous chapters, sometimes the WRB received rescue proposals from individuals. McClelland encountered one such proposal during the fall of 1944. Isaac Sternbuch, a member of the Swiss Vaad Hatzala Rescue Committee, got in touch with Jean-Marie Musy, the former president of Switzerland and a personal acquaintance of high-ranking Nazi Heinrich Himmler. Through Musy, Sternbuch's organization hoped to convince the Nazis that releasing the Jews so close to the end of the war was in Germany's best interest. Initially Sternbuch did not reveal his plans to McClelland. When McClelland learned that Musy had met with Himmler to discuss the release of "a considerable number of Jews" in exchange for money, McClelland advised the Board not to support the deal.[42] McClelland's concerns were twofold: he questioned Musy's reputation and he worried about the lack of details included in the so-called deal. Sternbuch's organization took a risk by involving Musy—he was pro-Nazi and admitted that he did not like Jews. Still, Musy had access to Himmler, and even if his motives were to help the Nazis save face at the end of the war, Sternbuch and his

---

40 Telegram to American Embassy in Rome from McClelland, 20 July 1945; Folder: Jews in Hungary and Bergen-Belsen Group: July–Dec. 1945; General Correspondence of R. McClelland; Papers of the War Refugee Board; Franklin D. Roosevelt Library, Hyde Park, NY.

41 Ibid.

42 Telegram to WRB from McClelland, 9 December 1944: Folder: Union of Orthodox Rabbis: Representation in Switzerland (I. Sternbuch), July–Dec.1944; General Correspondence of R. McClelland; Papers of the War Refugee Board; Franklin D. Roosevelt Library, Hyde Park, NY.

supporters wanted to rescue Jews at any cost. Jewish organizations like Vaad Hatzala backed up their convictions with money. They sent Sternbuch Swiss francs whenever he thought there was a chance to buy out Jews. In contrast, in January of 1945, McClelland remained "on the fence" in regard to Musy's negotiations with Himmler.[43]

After his third meeting with Himmler in February, Musy reported that Himmler had agreed to send all of the Jews in German-controlled territory to Switzerland at regular intervals if 5 million francs were placed in a Swiss bank in Musy's name.[44] To strengthen his credibility, Himmler promised Musy that a train of Jews would arrive in Switzerland soon. Sternbuch asked McClelland to intercede with the Swiss authorities so the first group of 1,200 Jews could be admitted.[45] Though skeptical of Himmler's promise to send Jews to Switzerland, McClelland contacted the Swiss police. When he encountered Swiss reluctance to take in refugees on a permanent basis, McClelland indicated that the United States would find a way to evacuate them.[46] To McClelland's credit, he had no idea whether the United States government supported his statement until he asked and received an affirmative reply days later. As a devoted refugee worker, McClelland decided to safeguard potential refugees, even if he thought they might not arrive.

While waiting to see if any refugees came to Switzerland, Mc-Clelland spent his time in an unproductive debate over whether or not Musy really needed the 5 million francs. First, McClelland worried that Musy might spend it himself, and then he wondered why someone like Himmler would find such a small sum sufficient if he

43   Telegram to WRB from McClelland, 27 January 1945; Folder: Union of Orthodox Rabbis: Representation in Switzerland (I. Sternbuch), January–June 1945; General Correspondence of R. McClelland; Papers of the War Refugee Board; Franklin D. Roosevelt Library, Hyde Park, NY.

44   Memo by McClelland on Sternbuch-Musy-Himmler Jewish Affair, 6 February 1945; Folder: Union of Orthodox Rabbis: Representation in Switzerland (I. Sternbuch), January–June 1945; General Correspondence of R. McClelland; Papers of the War Refugee Board; Franklin D. Roosevelt Library, Hyde Park, NY.

45   Ibid.

46   Ibid.

planned to release thousands of Jews.[47] If 5 million francs was in fact a small price to pay for saving lives, why did McClelland bother to question it? As seen in Chapter Five, the United States government avoided paying ransoms to the Axis powers. Even if ransom money might save lives, the government and the WRB balked at giving money to the enemy. Within the WRB, Henry Morgenthau in particular feared public opinion would turn against any rescue scheme if people discovered that the government paid money to the murderers of American soldiers.[48] Luckily McClelland found a way to provide Musy with the deposit without jeopardizing the American government's ransom policy. He proposed that the WRB place the funds in a joint account under Musy and McClelland's names.[49] That way Musy had to ask McClelland's permission before withdrawing money. The Board eventually approved the deal. In the meantime Sternbuch managed to borrow money from an unidentified source and place it in the Swiss account under Musy and McClelland's names.

Despite McClelland's doubts about Musy's motives and Himmler's promises, the Musy affair got results. McClelland reported to the WRB: "The German Legation at Bern informed the Federal Police at 6 p.m., February 6, that a convoy of 1,200 people was at Konstanz. The convoy came into Switzerland February 7 about noon. It is composed of 1,210 persons ... an unconfirmed report states that they came from Theresienstadt."[50] When the Jews' evacuation from Switzerland after the war was secured and the joint bank account had been approved by both the Board and the Treasury Department, McClelland hoped that more Jews would come to Switzerland.

---

47 Ibid.

48 Wyman, *The Abandonment*, 250.

49 Memo by McClelland on Sternbuch-Musy-Himmler Jewish Affair, 6 February 1945; Folder: Union of Orthodox Rabbis: Representation in Switzerland (I. Sternbuch), January–June 1945; General Correspondence of R. McClelland; Papers of the War Refugee Board; Franklin D. Roosevelt Library, Hyde Park, NY.

50 Telegram to WRB from McClelland, 8 February 1945; Folder: Union of Orthodox Rabbis: Representation in Switzerland (I. Sternbuch), January–June 1945; General Correspondence of R. McClelland; Papers of the War Refugee Board; Franklin D. Roosevelt Library, Hyde Park, NY.

Though Himmler and other Nazi officials thought shipping Jews to Switzerland was a practical move considering Germany's financial and military situation, Hitler disagreed. He had heard reports from the Swiss press about the release of certain Nazi detainees, including the Jews from Theresienstadt concentration camp. A WRB memo stated that "Hitler had immediately taken violent exception to any such step, particularly as regards Jews, and had a few days later summoned Himmler ... to a special meeting where Hitler definitely vetoed the evacuation or release from Germany of any of these people."[51] Himmler and the others at the meeting had little choice but to follow their leader, regardless of their opinions. To do otherwise would have resulted in their deaths. Musy tried to keep the negotiations with Himmler going and successfully prodded him to treat the concentration camp inmates more humanely, in contrast to Hitler's wishes.[52] No additional Jews reached Switzerland under the Musy affair, however.

With the help of Swiss authorities, and sometimes in spite of the authorities, McClelland accomplished much during his tenure as WRB representative. Through McClelland, trapped Jews in Italy and France received WRB funds to help them survive. Although he hesitated to involve the WRB in outright ransom schemes, McClelland supported rescue efforts, which included small-scale bribery of authority figures and contributions to underground Jewish organizations like Hechaluz. Even when he doubted the efficacy of a rescue scheme like Sternbuch and Musy's, McClelland still used his influence to persuade Swiss officials to admit more refugees just in case they arrived. Still, like most of the WRB's representatives, he wished he could have done more to save the Jews. In a summary of the Swiss mission's activities, McClelland wrote, "its successes

---

51 Memo by McClelland on conversation with Musy concerning his most recent trip to Germany, 9–10 April 1945; Folder: Union of Orthodox Rabbis: Representation in Switzerland (I. Sternbuch), January–June 1945; General Correspondence of R. McClelland; Papers of the War Refugee Board; Franklin D. Roosevelt Library, Hyde Park, NY.

52 Ibid.

were slight in relation to the frightful casualties sustained; yet it is sincerely felt that its accomplishments constitute a victory, small in comparison to that far greater one carried by force of arms, but which nevertheless adds a measure of particularly precious strength to our cause."[53]

---

53   *Report on the Activities of the WRB through its Representation at the American Legation in Bern, Switzerland, March 1944–July 1945*; Folder: Programs with Respect to Relief and Rescue of Refugees: Evacuations to and through Switzerland; General Correspondence of R. McClelland; Papers of the War Refugee Board; Franklin D. Roosevelt Library, Hyde Park, NY.

CHAPTER TEN

A One-man Rescue Operation: Raoul Wallenberg

ON JUNE 9, 1944, WRB representative Iver Olsen met a young businessman at the Hotel Saltsjöbaden in Sweden. The young man's business partner, Kalman Lauer, introduced the pair to each other. Lauer knew that the War Refugee Board was looking for someone to help rescue Jews who remained alive in Hungary. The junior partner had many of the traits Olsen sought, including Swedish ancestry, familiarity with Budapest, and an understanding of various foreign languages. Above all, however, Raoul Wallenberg possessed a talent for handling dangerous situations calmly. During summer breaks from college Wallenberg hitchhiked across the United States. On one occasion, the person who picked him up held him at gunpoint and demanded money. Wallenberg gave him some cash, but his calm demeanor frightened the robber so much that he let Wallenberg go unharmed.[1] Therefore, when Olsen explained the plight of Hungarian Jews, no one who knew Wallenberg was surprised that he jumped at the chance to put himself in danger for their benefit.

While his efforts on behalf of the Board are now legendary, Wallenberg was not an official member of the Board. As noted in Chapter Six, Pehle requested the neutrals to increase their presence in Hungary. Wallenberg and Olsen, Sweden's WRB representative, met following his request. According to the WRB's *Final Summary Report*: "The Board furnished Wallenberg detailed plans of action,

---

1 Raoul Wallenberg, Letter to Grandfather from Ann Arbor, 27 June 1933, reprinted in *Raoul Wallenberg: Letters and Dispatches 1924–1944*, trans. Kjersti Board (New York: Arcade Publishing, Inc., 1995), 92.

but made it clear that he could not act in Hungary as a representative of the Board."[2] Instead, the Swedish Foreign Office assigned Wallenberg as an Attaché to its Legation in Budapest. His task was to initiate relief for Hungarian Jews. Although these instructions make the Board's role in Wallenberg's subsequent rescue attempts seem negligible, the WRB provided Wallenberg with over $100,000 for rescue purposes along with a list of Hungarian officials who accepted bribes.[3] Olsen also stayed in touch with Wallenberg and convinced the WRB to send him additional funds when needed. Despite the Board's financial support, Wallenberg's task would not be an easy one.

One obstacle was in place before Wallenberg alighted from his train in Budapest. Like the Jewish community in Sweden, Hungary's general populace remained indifferent to the Jews' plight. Based on a conversation with a Hungarian informer, Olsen estimated that 80 percent of Hungarians were unmoved by the persecution of the Jews, while others were too intimidated by the Nazi regime, which had occupied the country in March, to aid the Jews.[4] The indifference to their fate led to deportations of Jews living in the Hungarian countryside during the spring and fall of 1944. If the Nazis eliminated the Jews in Budapest, there would be no work for Wallenberg to accomplish. Under such conditions, the "relentless campaign" that Wallenberg waged on behalf of Budapest's remaining 230,000 Jews seemed miraculous.[5]

Wallenberg's arrival at the Swedish Embassy in Hungary belied his status as a diplomat. Since he was in too great a hurry to start his work to make a reservation, Wallenberg spent the train ride to Budapest sitting on the floor, studying the WRB's list of possible contacts in Hungary. His luggage consisted of two knapsacks, a sleeping bag, and

---

2   *Final Summary Report of the Executive Director, War Refugee Board*, 15 September 1945, Papers of the War Refugee Board.

3   Feingold, 257–8.

4   Excerpts from Letter from Iver Olsen, WRB Representative in Stockholm, 10 August 1944, Papers of the War Refugee Board.

5   *Final Summary Report of the Executive Director, War Refugee Board*, 15 September 1945, Papers of the War Refugee Board.

a revolver.[6] In spite of his unprofessional appearance, Wallenberg at once took over the Jewish rescue operation. Within a few weeks he had set up an office and recruited Jewish volunteers to help him. Their primary task was to help Wallenberg process applications for Swedish protective passports.

At first Wallenberg hoped to save Jews by transporting them from Hungary to Sweden. Several hundred Jews already held Swedish passports, so evacuation, at least in theory, looked like a viable option. Soon, however, Wallenberg realized that he needed to come up with another solution. Securing German transit permits, for example, proved to be an obstacle to bringing Hungarian Jews to Sweden.[7] Still, Wallenberg never gave up on his mission to save Jews. Any Hungarian Jew with ties to Sweden through family members, business, or any other means received a Swedish protective passport. Some of these Jews had only tentative ties to Sweden, but technicalities made no difference to Wallenberg. Over time, he and his employees printed Swedish protective passports for 5,000 Jews.[8] The documents appeared very official and were signed by the foreign minister of Sweden. Each passport read: "The Royal Swedish Legation in Budapest certifies that the above-signed will be traveling to Sweden with the Royal Swedish Foreign Ministry's authorization … Until departure, he and his living quarters fall under the protection of the Royal Swedish Legation in Budapest."[9] Possession of these papers allowed most of the bearers to remain unmolested by Hungarian officials, but neither they nor the Nazis could be trusted.

Aware that the Nazis might still target Jews with Swedish papers, Wallenberg sought even greater protection for them. By using WRB

---

6   Per Anger, introduction to Dispatches from Budapest July 18–December 12, 1944 in
      Raoul Wallenberg: Letters and Dispatches, 222.
7   Telegram to secretary of state, Washington, from Johnson in Stockholm, 25 July 1944,
      Papers of the War Refugee Board.
8   Per Anger, introduction to Dispatches from Budapest July 18–December 12, 1944 in
      Raoul Wallenberg: Letters and Dispatches, 222.
9   Copy of Schutzpass for Ladielaus Gold, September 1944, as reproduced in *Raoul
      Wallenberg: Letters and Dispatches 1924–1944*.

funds, Wallenberg started acquiring apartments that served as safe houses for Jews who possessed Swedish identification. In addition to those with passports, other Jews were smuggled into the Swedish houses. The number of Jews under Swedish protection eventually rose to 15,000–20,000 thanks to Wallenberg's exploits.[10]

Wallenberg also used his considerable negotiating skills to gain better treatment for Jews. For example, he made a deal with the Hungarian government that his employees, most of whom were Jewish, did not have to wear the Jewish star.[11] Without that requirement, the nearly four hundred people eventually employed by Wallenberg avoided anti-Jewish measures such as curfews. He also enabled many other Jews to escape deportation by getting the Hungarian government to respect his protective passports, at least for the most part. Unlike some of his WRB counterparts who found arguing distasteful, Wallenberg took pleasure in his role as negotiator. In a letter to his mother, Wallenberg indicated that he often traveled in his car to visit various Nazi and Hungarian officials and "enjoy[ed] these negotiations very much."[12] Though he understood the seriousness of the Jews' situation, Wallenberg relished the chance to outwit his opponents. More often than not, Wallenberg emerged triumphant from his meetings with authority figures. In September, he wrote to his mother, "About a week ago, I took my official car, a rented Studebaker, and went to an internment camp on the Austrian border. The commandant refused to receive me at first, then he allotted me five minutes, and finally, after negotiating for four hours, I managed to have eighty people released the very same day."[13] Wallenberg's pride in his accomplishment was as evident in this note as his letter to his

---

10   Per Anger, introduction to Dispatches from Budapest July 18–December 12, 1944 in *Raoul Wallenberg: Letters and Dispatches*, 222.

11   Raoul Wallenberg, Dispatch from Budapest, 29 September 1944, reprinted in *Raoul Wallenberg: Letters and Dispatches*, 259.

12   Raoul Wallenberg letter to mother from Budapest, 29 September 1944, reprinted in *Raoul Wallenberg, Letters and Dispatches*, 275.

13   Ibid.

grandfather describing how he outsmarted the would-be robber as a student. Yet Wallenberg soon discovered that he needed to do more than arrange meetings if he wanted to save Budapest's Jews.

In mid-October 1944, the changing political situation in Hungary tested Wallenberg's resolve to continue his mission. Though Hungarian regent Horthy halted the deportation of Jews prior to Wallenberg's arrival, the Nazis installed a new government, led by the Arrow Cross, when they realized Horthy sought armistice with the Allies. The Arrow Cross engaged in terrorism against the Jews. Worst of all, the protective passports that Wallenberg had convinced the Horthy regime to recognize were considered worthless by the Arrow Cross.[14] Confident as ever in his ability to make a deal, Wallenberg met with Arrow Cross leader Ferenc Szálasi. He returned from his conference with Szálasi's written assurance that not only were Swedish passports valid and must be respected by authorities, but that the documents of other neutral legations such as Switzerland were also valid.[15]

Despite assurances to the contrary, the Hungarian government still threatened Jews who Wallenberg tried to protect. On one occasion the Hungarian military rounded up able-bodied Jewish men at Wallenberg's apartment complex and informed him that the Jews had to report for duty at labor camps.[16] Unlike his WRB counterparts, who primarily used diplomacy to get results, Wallenberg never hesitated to become directly involved with a rescue effort. Although the patrol was armed and he was not, Wallenberg insisted that the Arrow Cross leave Swedish territory. When they refused, he told them, "None will leave this place. If you try to take anyone away you will have to answer to me. As long as I live none will be taken out of here. First you will have to shoot me."[17] The soldiers declined the offer to make Sweden an enemy by shooting one of its

---

14   "Swedish Achievements in Hungary," from Swedish Newspaper *Dagens Nyheter*, 6
        March 1945, Papers of the War Refugee Board.

15   Ibid.

16   Ibid.

17   Ibid.

representatives. Instead, Wallenberg met with the commandant and procured a letter stating that Jews under Swedish protection did not have to report for labor service.[18]

That night Wallenberg returned to the apartment complex to discover that a handful of Jews had been captured by the Arrow Cross during his absence and placed on a deportation train. Still undaunted, Wallenberg intercepted the German train and removed the Jews who had Swedish papers.[19] At all times Wallenberg demonstrated a fervent desire to rescue Jews, even if his efforts endangered his life.

Budapest's Jews were in more danger than ever during November 1944. Though the Nazis had fewer trains to transport Hungary's Jews to the death camps, they found other ways to kill Jews. For example, they forced 40,000 Hungarian Jews to march 120 miles on foot to the Hungary-Austria border.[20] Many died during the journey, some from exposure to the weather and others from Nazi gunshot wounds when they could not march any longer. Yet even this dire circumstance failed to keep Wallenberg from carrying out his mission. Per Anger, another Swedish Legation employee, stated, "Wallenberg and I set out by car along the route the Jews were being marched. We had the car full of food, which we succeeded in passing out despite such help being prohibited, but it did not go very far."[21] The Swedish Legation, including Wallenberg, needed to find another way to aid the Jews.

Once again Wallenberg utilized the acting skills that made him so effective in official negotiations. He personally intervened during the so-called death marches, taking anyone who had Swedish papers out of the line and bringing them back to Budapest. Unlike some German

---

18   Ibid.
19   Telegram to secretary of state, Washington, from Johnson in Stockholm, 7 March
      1945, Papers of the War Refugee Board.
20   Telegram to secretary of state, Washington, from Johnson in Stockholm, 22
      December 1944, Papers of the War Refugee Board.
21   Per Anger, introduction to Dispatches from Budapest July 18–December 12, 1944 in
      Raoul Wallenberg: Letters and Dispatches, 225.

officials, the Arrow Cross had no respect for Swedish protective passports. In January 1945 the Arrow Cross rounded up Jews from Swedish safe houses, including Alice Breuer and her husband, and forced them to march to the Danube. They intended to shoot the Jews and throw them in the river. What the Arrow Cross had not counted on, however, was Wallenberg's appearance in the middle of the night. He brandished a megaphone and demanded that the Swedish Jews be returned to him. Alice Breuer remembered, "To our astonishment, the executioners obeyed Wallenberg. He seemed very tall indeed—and strong. He radiated power and dignity."[22] Thanks to Wallenberg's determination, Alice, her husband, and others with Swedish passports escaped death that night.

Wallenberg also met the few trains that deported Jews from the Hungarian border to the Nazi death camps. Because he had lookouts at the deportation stations, Wallenberg had good information as to when a train was leaving. He halted trains, demanding that the occupants show their papers. Sometimes the Jews on board had only pieces of paper with a bit of Hungarian written on them, but Wallenberg managed to get them out anyway while the Nazis stood by, stunned at the bravado of the Swedish diplomat.[23] Despite the risks Wallenberg took to save lives, his official reports revealed little of his heroics. A December dispatch from Budapest simply stated, "By intervening in some way when the Jews were boarding the trains or being taken away, about 2,000 persons have been returned."[24] Results were what mattered to Wallenberg, not public acclaim.

In addition to his sensational rescues, Wallenberg also involved himself in more mundane tasks such as finding food and supplies for Hungary's Jews. As with his other projects, Wallenberg encountered

---

22   Erwin K. Koranyi, *Dreams and Tears* (Ontario: General Store Publishing House, 2006), 90; quoted in Alex Kershaw, *The Envoy* (Cambridge, MA: Da Capo Press, 2010), 146.

23   Per Anger, introduction to Dispatches from Budapest July 18–December 12, 1944 in *Raoul Wallenberg: Letters and Dispatches*, 230.

24   Raoul Wallenberg, Dispatch from Budapest, 12 December 1944, reprinted in *Raoul Wallenberg, Letters and Dispatches*, 267.

problems trying to do relief work. One major problem was funding. In one of his early dispatches, a frustrated Wallenberg wrote, "Relief activity has been initiated on a very limited scale. Money has been requested—but not obtained—from a religious organization that has been very active in aiding the Jews ... I can only regret that those who were most eager to send me here have not seemed to understand that funds are essential. There is endless suffering to try to ease in this place."[25] By autumn Wallenberg's relief projects had more support from a handful of sources, including the Red Cross as well as individual donors. The donations enabled Wallenberg to distribute funds for soup kitchens, clothing, and a bombed-out Jewish orphanage.[26] Wallenberg was determined to get as many supplies as possible for Hungary's Jews by whatever means he had at his disposal. For example, in successive messages he hounded the Ministry of Foreign Affairs to send clothes, citing the desperate need among the Jews for any such items the Ministry could find.[27] As usual, Wallenberg refused to wait for a response to his requests before trying to solve as many problems as possible on site. He helped install a department that distributed shoes to the needy and formed a working committee with the Red Cross in an effort to send food and medicine to Hungarian Jews in Germany.[28] Like Olsen in Sweden, Wallenberg and his staff participated in the Red Cross' opening of two Budapest hospitals for sick or wounded Jews. Though the dramatic rescues from transport trains and other dangerous places received more attention from the media and from historians, Wallenberg's relief activities enabled him to save additional numbers of Jews who might have starved or died from inadequate medical care without his intervention.

---

25   Raoul Wallenberg, Dispatch from Budapest, 29 July 1944, reprinted in *Raoul Wallenberg, Letters and Dispatches*, 245–6.

26   Raoul Wallenberg, Dispatch from Budapest, 29 September 1944, reprinted in *Raoul Wallenberg, Letters and Dispatches*, 258.

27   Raoul Wallenberg, Dispatch from Budapest, 12 October 1944, reprinted in *Raoul Wallenberg, Letters and Dispatches*, 261.

28   Ibid.

As the Red Army moved in on Budapest, other Swedish diplomats began to leave the area. The Arrow Cross cared little for diplomatic niceties during the days prior to the Soviet occupation of Hungary, and neutral diplomats who had helped Jews were in danger. Yet Wallenberg decided to stay with the Jews he had worked so hard to save until the Soviets arrived. He told his colleague Per Anger, "I'd never be able to go back to Stockholm without knowing that I'd done all a man could do to save as many Jews as possible."[29] Wallenberg hoped to work out plans with the Soviets for the future of the Jews he saved. After the Soviets finally arrived in Budapest in early 1945, they freed the Jews in the ghettos. They did not give the man who saved them the same privilege. Instead, the Russians believed Wallenberg was a German spy and arrested him. The Soviets viewed Wallenberg's claims that he met with German officials only to save Jews as "illogical."[30] None of them understood why a man of Wallenberg's wealth and neutral status chose to stay in such a dangerous place as Budapest. After being taken into Soviet custody, Wallenberg was never heard from again.[31]

The exact number of Budapest Jews that Wallenberg saved from extermination is unknown. Depending on the source, claims were made that he rescued between 20,000 and 100,000 Jews out of the 124,000 who survived in the city.[32] The *Final Summary Report* of the WRB stated, "[A]pproximately 20,000 Jews received the safety of Swedish protection in Hungary."[33] Wallenberg directly saved at least 20,000 Jews, but he likely saved thousands more indirectly by providing soup kitchens, medical care, and in some cases, giving hope to people who had given up on survival. An estimated

---

29 Per Anger, introduction to Dispatches from Budapest July 18–December 12, 1944 in *Raoul Wallenberg: Letters and Dispatches*, 229.

30 Kershaw, 179.

31 Telegram to secretary of state, Washington, from American Legation, Stockholm, 7 June 1945, Papers of the War Refugee Board.

32 Per Anger, introduction to Dispatches from Budapest July 18–December 12, 1944 in *Raoul Wallenberg: Letters and Dispatches*, 230.

33 *Final Summary Report of the Executive Director, War Refugee Board*, 15 September 1945, Papers of the War Refugee Board.

70,000 Jews survived the war in the Budapest ghetto.[34] Wallenberg helped many of them stay alive by providing them with the necessities they needed.

Although the survivors who credit Wallenberg with their rescue have different stories, they all agreed that Wallenberg's presence gave them hope for the future—something they had lost while being hunted down by the Nazis and later the Arrow Cross. Susan Tabor wrote about her experience of walking to the Austrian border, being shoved into a stable by Nazi guards, and then seeing Wallenberg enter the stable with other civilians. "The one holding the large book … apologized for not being able to save us all … He then asked us who had the Swedish safe pass to give them their names. My mother and I had no Schutzpass, but because of Raoul Wallenberg's compassion and concern, hope returned to my soul … As those few women with the safe pass walked out with Raoul Wallenberg, we joined them. When they climbed into the back of the Swede's truck, we ran into the woods and returned to Budapest on foot."[35] In the face of great adversity, some people lost their will to live. Though he could not save everyone directly, Wallenberg tried to ensure through his belief in the worthiness of Jewish lives that no one would stop fighting to live.

Wallenberg's most important achievement lies in the effect that his actions had on others. In addition to inspiring Jews to save themselves, he also influenced the Red Cross, the Swiss, Spanish, and Portuguese legations, and the papal nuncio to step up their rescue operations.[36] As a result of Wallenberg's influence, between 11,000 and 30,000 additional lives were saved by other groups.[37] His efforts also confirmed that the Jews could be rescued and silenced the naysayers. Historian Arthur Morse stated, "All those

---

34   Wyman, *The Abandonment*, 242.

35   Rachel Oestreicher Haspel, president of the Raoul Wallenberg Committee of the United States, afterword to *Raoul Wallenberg: Letters and Dispatches*, 283.

36   *Final Report of the Activities of the WRB from Sweden*, 15 June 1945, Papers of the War Refugee Board.

37   Wyman, *The Abandonment*, 242.

who had thrown up their hands in despair could no longer plead the impossibility of rescue, for Raoul Wallenberg provided daily proof of its feasibility. The War Refugee Board gave him the resources to do the job but his actions gave meaning to the very existence of the Board."[38] Wallenberg's successful rescues exposed the policy of Allied inaction as wholly without foundation and reaffirmed the ability of the WRB to rescue victims of enemy oppression. If the State Department in America had shown the same dedication to the plight of European Jews from the start of the Holocaust as Wallenberg did at the end, perhaps no Jews would have needed Wallenberg's protection in 1944.

---

38   Morse, 299.

CHAPTER ELEVEN

Excuses, Excuses: The War Department's Justifications for Not Bombing the Camps

ALTHOUGH THE WRB's FOREIGN REPRESENTATIVES often succeeded in prodding government officials in other countries to help refugees, its members in Washington struggled to achieve results. As mentioned in the executive order, the WRB's executive director had the authority, at least in theory, to enlist aid from the State, Treasury, and War Departments. In more than one instance, the State Department proved its determination to thwart WRB efforts at rescue. Yet State was not the only department that lacked interest in the refugee problem. During the summer of 1944, WRB Director John Pehle faced opposition from the War Department.

By June of 1944 the appeal to bomb the rail lines that led to Auschwitz was no longer a novel idea. The WRB received bombing requests from Jewish organizations in the spring but put little pressure on the War Department to act. When Pehle contacted Assistant Secretary of War John McCloy, Pehle stated that he was uncertain whether bombing rail lines would have any appreciable effect on deportations.[1] Pehle's doubts made it easy for the secretary to reject the idea. Yet in the summer, one telegram containing information on railways got Pehle's attention, perhaps because the WRB representative in Switzerland had sent it. Roswell McClelland's

---

1   Letter to Assistant Secretary of War John McCloy from John Pehle, 24 June 1944; Folder: Measures Directed Toward Halting Persecution Hungary, Vol. 5; Papers of the War Refugee Board, Franklin D. Roosevelt Library, Hyde Park, NY.

telegram included a list of railway lines and bridges Gerhart Riegner had received from sources in Slovakia and Hungary. McClelland stated that each line transported thousands of Jews per day to Nazi death camps.[2] Though McClelland refrained from commenting on the feasibility of the bombing proposal, the mere fact that he passed the information on to the WRB prompted Pehle to contact the War Department again.

Unsurprisingly, McCloy again rejected the idea of bombing rail lines. His reply to Pehle stated that the bombings "could be executed only by the diversion of considerable air support essential to the success of our forces now engaged in decisive operations and would in any case be of such doubtful efficacy that it would not amount to a practical project."[3] Whether or not bombing railway lines would have been effective in the long run is beyond the scope of this book. Others have argued that the Nazis had the skill to rebuild rail lines in a hurry. Yet McCloy's postwar actions indicate that he had other reasons besides manpower and the success of the project on his mind when he rejected the railway bombing proposals. In 1949 McCloy became United States Military Governor and High Commissioner for Germany. His Clemency Act of 1951 enabled many convicted Nazis to have their sentences significantly shortened.[4] If the WRB hoped to find someone in the War Department who was sympathetic to the Jews, McCloy was the wrong man.

Even if bombing rail lines was impractical, McClelland's telegram caused some Board members and Jewish groups to endorse a different plan—the bombing of the extermination camps. McClelland stated that since the summer of 1942 the Nazis had killed at least 1.5 million Jews, and the camps were already prepared in early 1944 to

---

2   Telegram to WRB from McClelland, 24 June 1944; Folder: Measures Directed Toward Halting Persecution Hungary, Vol. 5; Papers of the War Refugee Board, Franklin D. Roosevelt Library, Hyde Park, NY.

3   Letter to John Pehle from Assistant Secretary of War John McCloy, 4 July 1944; Folder: Measures Directed Toward Halting Persecution Hungary, Vol. 5; Papers of the War Refugee Board, Franklin D. Roosevelt Library, Hyde Park, NY.

4   Martin Gilbert, *Auschwitz and the Allies* (New York: Henry Holt and Co., 1981), 349.

exterminate Hungarian Jews.[5] After reading McClelland's telegram, WRB member Benjamin Akzin expressed his support for a mission to bomb the camps. In a WRB memo, Akzin wrote that the number of lives saved in such an operation would be "quite appreciable," as "with German manpower and material resources gravely depleted, German authorities might not be in a position to devote themselves to the task of equipping new large-scale extermination centers."[6] Compared to repairing railroad tracks, reconstructing the killing centers at Birkenau and Auschwitz would be far more complicated and time consuming. Bombing the camps had the added potential to kill some of the Nazis who carried out the killings. Akzin's memo never left WRB headquarters and his thoughts were not passed on to the War Department. Instead, other upper-level Board members sent McClelland's telegram to the Assistant Secretary of War, who had rejected the bombing of rail lines. McCloy did not mention the possibility of bombing the extermination camps in his reply, but the issue resurfaced throughout the summer and fall of 1944.

Akzin was not the only person who thought the camps at Auschwitz and Birkenau needed to be bombed. Jewish groups, one of which took its case directly to the president, also supported a bombing plan. In a letter to FDR, the Emergency Committee to Save the Jewish People of Europe advocated the bombing of the extermination centers. They received a reply from the State Department indicating that such a plan would "divert military energies" from the main objective of winning the war.[7] The group did not give up that easily, however. They again wrote to the

---

5   Telegram to WRB from McClelland, 24 June 1944; Folder: Measures Directed Toward Halting Persecution Hungary, Vol. 5; Papers of the War Refugee Board, Franklin D. Roosevelt Library, Hyde Park, NY.

6   WRB inter-office communication to L. S. Lesser from B. Akzin; Folder: Measures Directed Toward Halting Persecution Hungary, Vol. 5; Papers of the War Refugee Board, Franklin D. Roosevelt Library, Hyde Park, NY.

7   Letter to FDR from Executive Vice-Chairman of Emergency Committee to Save the Jewish People of Europe, 24 July 1944; Folder: Measures Directed Toward Halting Persecution Hungary, Vol. 5; Papers of the War Refugee Board, Franklin D. Roosevelt Library, Hyde Park, NY.

president and stated that bombing the camps "will not require any additional exertion of military forces nor call for any deviation from the successful military campaigns now in progress."[8] Though bias on the part of a group trying to save the lives of Jews would be understandable, the facts bear out the assertion that destroying Auschwitz and Birkenau was an achievable goal. The problem was that no one in authority wanted to achieve it.

While the State and War Departments denied the military's ability to bomb the camps, evidence shows that United States military planes were in the vicinity of Auschwitz. In fact one United States mission took place so close to Auschwitz and Birkenau that a small number of bombs were accidentally dropped on the camps. Since one of the military's goals was to disrupt German manufacturing in order to further deplete the enemy's war supplies, its leaders decided that the most effective way to stop the production of German goods was to bomb Axis factories. By taking photos of the surrounding area, the United States Air Force located synthetic oil plants like the IG Farben factory at Monowitz. Coincidently, one photo from June 26 included pictures of the gas chambers at Auschwitz and Birkenau.[9] Features from the camps stood out, including the gas chambers, the crematoria, and a train at Birkenau. Of course, the Air Force did not use the photo to bomb the camps. Its orders were to bomb the factory, not to eliminate the Nazi killing machines. On September 13, 1944, despite anti-aircraft fire, the Americans bombed the factory.[10] Monowitz lay only five miles from the gas chambers that continued to kill thousands of Jews each day. By accident, the pilots dropped bombs on Birkenau, damaging a railway leading to the camp and the sides of the crematoria.[11] Bombs also fell on a portion of Auschwitz. Those bombs hit and destroyed SS barracks and killed fifteen SS men as well as twenty-three civilians.[12] One can

---

8   Ibid.
9   Gilbert, 250.
10   Ibid., 315.
11   Ibid.
12   Ibid.

only imagine how much more damage might have been done to the extermination centers if the military targeted them directly.

Until the fall of 1944, Benjamin Akzin was the only Board member who consistently pressed for the bombing of the camps and the rail lines leading to them. After reading what became known as the Vrba-Wetzler Report, the Board's executive director at last agreed with his colleague. In October McClelland sent the US government the complete text of the Vrba-Wetzler Report, which contained information about the camps of Auschwitz and Birkenau from two escaped prisoners.[13] The report made clear the elaborate structure of the gas chambers and crematoria, as well as their locations within the camps. Birkenau, for example, had four crematoria. The two largest consisted of three parts: the furnace room, the large hall where unsuspecting victims were told to undress for bathing, and the gas chamber. The daily killing capacity of all four cremating and gassing plants at Birkenau totaled about 6,000 people.[14]

Armed with the eyewitness reports, Pehle decided to appeal again to McCloy. In contrast to his previous messages, Pehle now gave his full support to the bombing of Auschwitz and Birkenau. He wrote, "Until now, despite pressure from many sources, I have been hesitant to urge the destruction of these camps by direct, military action. But I am convinced that the point has now been reached where such an action is justifiable ... I strongly recommend that the War Department give serious consideration to the possibility of destroying the execution chambers and crematories in Birkenau through direct bombing action."[15] As Akzin argued in his WRB memo months earlier, Pehle explained the difficulties the Nazis would encounter if they tried to rebuild the camps given the "elaborate murder installations" used to kill Jews.[16] Pehle's newfound

---

13   Transmission of two reports on the German concentration and extermination camps to Pehle from McClelland, 12 October 1944; Papers of the War Refugee Board.

14   Ibid.

15   Letter to John McCloy from John Pehle, 8 November 1944; Papers of the War Refugee Board.

16   Ibid.

enthusiasm for the bombing proposals came too late to influence anyone in the War Department. McCloy indicated that the best solution to the Jewish Problem was a swift end to the war. He also argued that bombing the camps would divert the US Air Force from its mission of destroying industrial targets "vital to the dwindling war potential of the enemy."[17] Ironically, as Pehle later discovered and as noted above, the United States Air Force managed to damage small sections of the camps while targeting Nazi manufacturing plants.

Why did Pehle fail to support the bombing of the camps even though the WRB had been receiving proposals from various sources for months? He and other members of the Treasury Department had previously put their reputations and jobs on the line by exposing the State Department's immigration policy to FDR in January, so it seemed logical that Pehle would support any means of stopping the killing of Jews. Yet when the opportunity arose to support the Jewish groups as well his colleague Benjamin Akzin on the bombing issue, Pehle hesitated.

In a contemporary interview, Pehle spoke about the eyewitness reports of Jewish persecution and extermination that reached the Board. He stated, "These reports give facts which none of us want to believe and which Americans naturally refuse to believe until overwhelming evidence has been presented. We on the War Refugee Board have been very skeptical. We remembered too well the atrocity stories of the last war, many of which were apparently untrue."[18] During World War I, the Americans and British engaged in propaganda against the Germans, accusing them of raping and killing women and children, as well as torturing POWs.[19] By spreading such tales, the United States and Britain hoped to encourage their

---

17 Letter to John Pehle from John McCloy, 18 November 1944; Papers of the War Refugee Board.

18 Pehle Interview with YANK's Washington Bureau, 7 November 1944; Papers of the War Refugee Board.

19 "The Chant of the German Sword," *New York Times Current History, October 1915–March 1916*, quoted in Ross F. Collins, *World War I: Primary Documents on Events from 1914–19* (West Port, CT: Greenwood Press, 2008), 52.

boys to fight harder against the supposedly evil Germans. Prior to US entry into World War II, some Americans thought that Jewish sympathizers exaggerated the most extreme examples of Nazi torture against the Jews in order to spur America's entrance into the war. Yet any exaggeration of the Nazis' brutality against the Jews made little sense considering the high rate of anti-Semitism in the United States and Britain. Few men in either country would fight harder to save an unpopular minority. Nevertheless, even well-meaning men like Pehle were human beings who did not always use logic when confronted with the horrors of the Holocaust.

In addition to Pehle's doubts about Nazi atrocities, his telegrams to McCloy reveal his discomfort with telling the War Department what steps it should take regarding any bombing plans. Because he was not a military man, Pehle thought he should defer to McCloy when it came to the feasibility of bombing a rail line or a death camp. He told the media that "any civilian naturally hesitates to try to tell a soldier the nature of the enemy which he is fighting."[20] Unfortunately, Assistant Secretary of War McCloy's postwar activities proved that he was biased against the Jews and would have been unlikely to bomb the camps even if he had formed a viable plan. Pehle, of course, did not know McCloy's true attitude toward the Jews and mistakenly trusted him to make impartial decisions on bombing requests.

Though Pehle erred by failing to support bombing proposals sooner, he did not hesitate to share with the public eyewitness accounts of the atrocities committed at Auschwitz and Birkenau. Via McClelland the WRB received eyewitness testimony from two Slovakian Jews who managed to escape the camps (the Vrba-Wetzler Report) and from a non-Jewish Polish major from Auschwitz. The reports left little to the imagination in their descriptions of Nazi brutality. One escapee described a transport of Polish Jews who arrived at Auschwitz: "They had received no water for days and when

---

20   Pehle Interview with YANK's Washington Bureau, 7 November 1944; Papers of the
      War Refugee Board.

the doors of the freight cars were opened we were ordered to chase them out with loud shouts. They were utterly exhausted and about a hundred of them had died during the journey. The living were lined up in rows of five … a commission from the political department proceeded with the selection of approximately 10% of the men and 5% of the women and had them transferred to the camps. The remainder were loaded on trucks, sent to Birkenau, and gassed while the dead and dying were taken directly to the furnaces."[21] The Board members placed their confidence in the reports, stating in a press release scheduled for November 26, 1944 that "The Board has every reason to believe that these reports present a true picture of the frightful happenings in these camps. It is making the reports public in the firm conviction that they should be read and understood by all Americans."[22] In Pehle's opinion and that of others on the Board, the American public was entitled to know the nature of the enemy that American soldiers were fighting. Prominent newspapers agreed and they released the text of the report in full.

Not everyone in authority thought the reports should be publicized. In particular the director of the Office of War Information, Elmer Davis, objected to the WRB press release. Objections were linked to fears of possible Nazi reprisals on American soldiers due to the WRB's condemnation of war criminals.[23] Since Pehle had not bothered to clear the press release with the OWI or the Departments of State and War, the agency's opposition made no difference. Nevertheless, Pehle made a point of refuting the OWI's objections in a meeting with Davis. He reminded the OWI that it had published FDR's statement of March 24, which condemned Nazi crimes against Jews. Pehle also stated, "[T]here was considerable doubt in

---

21   Transmission of two reports on the German concentration and extermination camps to Pehle from McClelland, 12 October 1944; Papers of the War Refugee Board.

22   WRB Press Release German Extermination Camps—Auschwitz and Birkenau, to be Released 26 November 1944; Papers of the War Refugee Board.

23   WRB memo to files regarding Mr. Elmer Davis' questioning of War Refugee Board's release of German atrocity stories, 22 November 1944; Papers of the War Refugee Board.

people's minds as to whether anything actually was going to be done about war criminals."[24] Whether Pehle intended to use the atrocity report as evidence of war crimes at this point cannot be determined. Yet when the war ended, WRB members exerted great influence not only over the punishments of war criminals but also on a new definition of war crimes.

---

24   Ibid.

CHAPTER TWELVE

Free Ports for Humans: Fort Ontario

ON A SUMMER DAY IN 1944, a ship named the *Henry Gibbins* arrived on the shores of New York. Nine hundred eighty-six refugees watched as the ship passed the Statue of Liberty. They originated from eighteen different countries, spoke different languages, and some of their religions differed. One young woman arrived wearing only a long shirt that her father had given to her before he was deported, while others had a few possessions. Each refugee had one thing in common, however: they had all survived Nazi Europe and they all came to America at the invitation of the president of the United States.

Members of the War Refugee Board recognized early on that other nations would not be motivated to take in refugees unless the United States relaxed its own strict immigration policy. Any policy changes needed to satisfy restrictionists in Congress, who insisted that the immigration laws stay in place, and at the same time save lives by allowing more refugees to enter the country. Samuel Grafton, a columnist for the *New York Post*, proposed the idea of free ports for refugees. In his April 5, 1944 column, he suggested that the practice of allowing parcels to lie duty-free in certain ports while awaiting shipment could be adapted to humans. The human "cargo" that arrived from Europe could be sent to abandoned army posts or internment camps. While these locations were hardly ideal, they were preferable to concentration camps or the gas chambers. As Grafton wrote, "The time is so short, our current example to the world is so bad, that it is necessary to settle for whatever can be done."[1]

Refugee groups sprung into action and urged FDR to approve the free port idea. The Emergency Committee to Save the Jewish People of Europe circulated a petition in support of the free ports. The WRB files contain many copies of this petition, signed by hundreds of Americans. It stated, "We the undersigned Americans do hereby petition the President to establish, without delay, temporary Rescue Camps within the United States ... to open these 'free ports' of hope and encouragement to those Jewish people who can flee Nazi murder squads, and to give them sanctuary therein until the coming peace."[2] Fortunately for the Emergency Committee and its supporters, the idea of free ports for refugees captured the attention of government officials.

In particular, WRB Director John Pehle worked tirelessly to translate Grafton's notion into reality. He held a special news conference explaining the rationale behind the so-called free port plan, and both he and Secretary Morgenthau pressured Roosevelt to establish a free port via executive order.[3] In Pehle's opinion, the WRB could not expect cooperation from other nations on the refugee issue unless the United States set the example. Pehle felt both pleased and disappointed when FDR announced to Congress on June 12, 1944 that a maximum of 1,000 refugees of various ethnic groups would arrive at Fort Ontario in Oswego, New York.[4] Although he wanted to rescue more refugees, Pehle and other refugee advocates hoped the camp would be the first of many havens in the United States.

The American public's reaction to the president's message was mixed. Multiple folders in the WRB files contain letters from

---

1   Ruth Gruber, *Haven: The Unknown Story of 1,000 World War II Refugees* (New York: Coward-McCann, 1983), 38.
2   Petition to Franklin D. Roosevelt from Emergency Committee to Save the Jewish People of Europe; Folder: Admission of Refugees to the U.S. (Free Ports); Papers of the War Refugee Board; Franklin D. Roosevelt Library, Hyde Park, NY.
3   Feingold, 263.
4   Friedman, 29.

individual Americans urging FDR to open more refugee camps. The Emergency Committee's Youth Division created small slips of paper which stated that the president would have the support of most Americans if he opened additional camps for Hitler's victims.[5] Supporters cut the slips of paper out of newspapers and other publications, added their signatures, and mailed them to the White House. Although the sheer volume of these messages attest to the willingness of many to take in more refugees, other Americans protested the idea of additional refugees entering the country. Mrs. Leonard Watkins from Colorado wrote to her senator, "They [the refugees] will never go back—and in a few years they will be so strong in numbers—we can do nothing about Keep[ing] America for Americans."[6] Mrs. Watkins and others, though descended from immigrants, did not want additional refugees coming to America, particularly if the refugees were Jewish. On at least one occasion, anti-immigrant sentiments reached the WRB in the form of a veiled threat. The Board received a telegram in July 1944 that stated, "If you admit one more refugee you will deserve, and receive, the hatred of all future generations."[7] In case Board members or the president had forgotten, such messages reminded them that American anti-Semitism still existed.

In Italy, the country from which FDR chose to accept refugees, the news that the United States had decided to open its doors slightly to the victims of Nazism spread like wildfire. Max Perlman, a representative of the American Jewish Joint Distribution Committee in Italy, helped select the refugees who later referred to themselves as the chosen ones. Perlman said, "Day and night, people

---

5   Emergency Committee Slip Signed by Gertrude Hausen to the President: Folder: Emergency Refugee Shelter Approval; Papers of the War Refugee Board; Franklin D. Roosevelt Library, Hyde Park, NY.

6   Letter from Mrs. Leonard Watkins to Senator Johnson, 15 June 1944; Folder: Emergency Refugee Shelter Disapproval; Papers of the War Refugee Board; Franklin D. Roosevelt Library, Hyde Park, NY.

7   Telegram from G. Robinson to WRB, 22 July 1944; Folder: Emergency Refugee Shelter Disapproval; Papers of the War Refugee Board; Franklin D. Roosevelt Library, Hyde Park, NY.

were knocking on the doors of all the offices taking applications ... women and men weeping, people fainting from emotion, parents holding their children up in the air so we'd notice them ... We were playing God to a group of desperate people."[8] Since FDR stipulated that only 1,000 people could immigrate to the United States, many others were turned away. In all, 3,000 people applied for a chance to enter the land of the free.[9]

The job of administrating Fort Ontario lay with the Department of the Interior. Secretary of the Interior Harold Ickes felt that someone from the government should meet the refugees on the ship and prepare them to come to America. He wanted to send Ruth Gruber, a young woman who served as his special assistant in the department for three years. Like many of the refugees, Gruber spoke German and Yiddish. She also shared Ickes' passion for rescuing European Jews. At first, some people doubted that a woman could undertake such a dangerous mission or command the respect from refugees that a man would. Ultimately, John Pehle of the WRB communicated with the Interior Department and gave his approval for Gruber to leave.[10] As a precaution, Gruber held the rank of simulated general in case the Nazis took her prisoner en route to Italy. Fortunately, she arrived safely to greet the refugees and help them during their journey.

Yet even when the chosen refugees finally reached Fort Ontario, they were not truly free. Hysterical refugees panicked when they saw the fence surrounding the fort. So many of them had survived concentration camps only to be forced behind another fence. Ruth Gruber, who gained the trust of the refugees during the perilous voyage, tried to assure them that they were safe, but many did not believe her.[11] With very few exceptions, refugees were not allowed to leave the camp. Nor were they given any assurances that they could someday apply for American citizenship. Upon their arrival, John

---

8   Gruber, 65.
9   Ibid.
10   Gruber, 21.
11   Gruber, 151.

Pehle stated that the refugees "will be housed and cared for at Fort Ontario, under adequate security precautions, until the war is over and they can return to their homes."[12] Thus while the refugees were temporarily safe, their future remained unclear.

Despite their uncertain future, the refugees enjoyed some small pleasures that they did not possess while under Nazi rule. Whereas the concentration camps offered no privacy, at Fort Ontario each family had a small "apartment" furnished with two metal cots, a small table, two chairs, and an army locker.[13] One of the refugees confided to Ruth Gruber that he used to dream about sleeping on his own mattress. Another woman cried when she discovered that the cots had bed sheets.[14]

For the young people, one pleasure of Fort Ontario included the opportunity to leave the camp on school days. Attending school was not an option in the concentration camps. In Oswego, however, the principals of the town's public schools welcomed the refugees. The idea of going to school intimidated some of the children. Few of them knew how to speak or write English. Yet many of the new students adjusted very well, especially those attending high school. Teachers reported to parents that the students were eager to learn, and some applied themselves more vigorously than their American classmates. For example, high school student Ernst Spitzer's classmates teased him by complaining that he studied too hard. He replied, "In prison camp, I was too hungry to study."[15] Their high school experiences transformed the lives of many Fort Ontario youth. Several students found their future vocation in engineering when the school's shop teacher took a group of students on a field trip to see local industrial plants.[16]

Although children and teenagers left the camp for school several

---

12   Statement by John Pehle, Executive Director of the WRB, to be Released on Arrival of the Refugees, no date; Papers of the War Refugee Board.

13   Gruber, 155.

14   Ibid.

15   Gruber, 206.

16   Ibid., 205–6.

days a week, adults remained inside the camp at all times. Jewish and refugee charitable agencies decided that adults would benefit from taking classes in order to relieve the monotony. Many of the refugees wished to improve their English, so the agencies provided English courses inside the camp. Soon other classes were added, including carpentry, jewelry making, and even beauty classes.[17] Edith Semjen, a young woman who had dropped out of high school, walked into a beauty course and discovered what she wanted to do with her life. The other women in the camp praised Edith's skills and soon she accumulated a long list of clients who wanted her to style their hair.[18]

Despite the positive aspects of life at Fort Ontario, living in a refugee camp remained far from ideal. The United States Department of Justice refused to recognize the refugees as aliens, which would at least have given them the legal status of prisoners of war.[19] Without any legal status, refugees, unlike Nazi POWs, had no opportunity to work outside the camp. Israel Willner, a cook in the fort's kosher kitchen, learned that chefs in the town of Oswego earned $500 per month. He said, "I want to go out and work and make something of myself. I have a visa to the United States in my pocket, and now I am wasting my life."[20] In addition to not being permitted to take up jobs, their lack of legal status prevented refugees with family living in America from visiting their loved ones, even if the relatives lived nearby. Refugees could roam around Oswego for a maximum of six hours, but even that privilege required special permission.[21] Some of the younger refugees found ways to bypass the strict regulations, though. For example, two of the young men crawled under the fence and explored the town on several occasions.[22]

In September, First Lady Eleanor Roosevelt visited the camp, where she witnessed the relief and the frustration of its inhabitants.

---

17   Ibid., 216.
18   Ibid.
19   Ibid., 167.
20   Ibid., 232–3.
21   Ibid., 217.
22   Ibid.

On a visit to the camp hospital, she met a young patient named David Levy. Mrs. Roosevelt asked him how he liked the camp. He said he loved America and the camp but wanted to go to college. As camp director Joe Smart explained, he was unable to enroll any refugees in the State Teachers College because of logistical problems. Mrs. Roosevelt told Smart, "For the sake of these young people, I hope you will find a way. If you need my help, please write me."[23] Mrs. Roosevelt did not forget her trip to Fort Ontario. In February 1945 David Levy and a small group of other refugees entered the doors of the Oswego State Teachers College for the spring semester.[24]

Short trips to the outside world failed to alleviate the refugees' frustration with their confinement, particularly those who could not attend school. One refugee, Dr. Ernst Wolff, wrote the following in a letter to Ruth Gruber: "I am told we refugees are prisoners because we have not status under the law: So we exist in a legal vacuum, under a sentence more cruel than that of a common criminal—the sentence of uncertainty ... For what freedom is America fighting a war abroad only to lose it in shame in Fort Ontario?"[25] Though they had arrived in America and were saved from the Nazi death camps, the refugees at Fort Ontario still felt insecure. They had good reason to be concerned. The executive order, which allowed them to enter the United States, also promised that they would be sent back to their home countries after the war.[26] Considering the many bombings of European towns, refugees and those who worked with them questioned whether the population of Fort Ontario would have homes to which they could return.

Ruth Gruber and other refugee workers lobbied current and former WRB members to allow the refugees to stay in the United States. They visited Secretary Morgenthau, who felt that he must

23   Gruber, 210.
24   Ibid., 226.
25   Ibid., 224.
26   Statement by John Pehle, Executive Director of the War Refugee Board, to be Released on Arrival of the Refugees, no date; Papers of the War Refugee Board.

honor FDR's statement that the refugees would return to Europe, even though the president had died.[27] John Pehle, who attended the meeting despite the fact that he was no longer director of the WRB, nodded in silent agreement. Back in June of 1944, Pehle promised a senator who received letters opposing the influx of refugees from his constituents that the immigration laws would not be altered to accommodate them.[28] Pehle chose not to change his position as the fate of the fort's inhabitants hung in the balance. Instead, he and Morgenthau suggested that Congress decide the fate of the Fort Ontario refugees.[29] Refugee advocates harbored no illusions about Congress' sentiment for immigrants, especially Jewish ones. A visit to the fort by a group of congressmen converted some to the refugee cause, but the converts failed to overcome the objections of the isolationists. Camp director Joe Smart formed a committee of one hundred prominent leaders, including Eleanor Roosevelt, who sought to keep the refugees in America.[30] Discouraged but not yet defeated, Gruber and others waited for an announcement from the one man who could change the fate of the inmates at Fort Ontario: President Harry Truman.

On December 22, 1945 Ruth Gruber listened to President Truman's radio broadcast in her Washington, DC apartment. Truman began by stating that the immigration quotas would not be changed. Gruber's heart sank. She thought the refugees had no hope of staying in the country without an alteration of the quotas.[31] Yet Truman's broadcast also addressed the difficulties facing the refugees in Fort Ontario. Since most of their homelands lay in ruins, Truman stated, "It would be inhumane and wasteful to require these people to go all the way back to Europe merely

---

27   Gruber, 242.
28   Letter to Senator Johnson from John Pehle, 15 June 1944; Folder: Emergency
      Refugee Shelter Disapproval; Papers of the War Refugee Board; Franklin D.
      Roosevelt Library, Hyde Park, NY.
29   Gruber, 243.
30   Ibid., 263.
31   Ibid., 270.

for the purpose of applying there for immigration visas ... I am therefore directing the Secretary of State and the Attorney General to adjust the immigration status of the members of this group who may wish to stay here, in strict accordance with existing laws."[32] Refugee advocates and the refugees themselves rejoiced at the news. The former aliens were no longer just Americanized—they were now Americans.

Social workers arrived at Fort Ontario to help the former refugees transition to civilian life. Seventy communities across the country offered to welcome the new Americans by finding them housing and jobs, as well as schools for their children.[33] Whereas before they could not even leave the fort for a short visit, any refugees with relatives in the United States were now allowed to join them. Magrita Ehrenstamm's daughter rented an apartment for her in New York before she arrived. While she packed at the fort, Magrita said, "I still can't believe this—that I'll have a kitchen of my own and privacy."[34] On January 17, 1946, the first three busloads of refugees left the fort.[35] At last the former camp inmates could start rebuilding their lives as free people.

Most of the young refugees took advantage of the opportunities for advancement in America. By working during the day and going to school at night, Paul Bokros finally realized his Oswego High School dream of becoming an engineer for defense and space programs.[36] Edith Semjen, who trained as a hairdresser through the beauty courses offered at Fort Ontario, opened her own beauty salon in New York City.[37] Other former refugees studied to become lawyers, teachers, rabbis, and doctors. These young men and women all felt gratitude to the country that took them in when they had nothing and later allowed them to flourish. Alex Margulis, a

---

32   Ibid., 271.
33   Ibid., 274.
34   Ibid.
35   Ibid.
36   Ibid., 300.
37   Ibid., 291.

graduate of Harvard who helped develop the CAT scanner, stated that "As I look back, I think Oswego was one of my most wonderful experiences ... the young people were happy. They felt it was an island of plenty."[38] Given the accomplishments of the few people who found refuge in Fort Ontario, one can only wonder what the refugees who never received visas to the United States might have contributed to American society.

To the extent that it encouraged a generation of young men and women from Hitler's Europe to become better educated and self-sufficient, Fort Ontario was a success. Yet members of the WRB hoped from the beginning that by opening free ports to refugees, the United States would inspire other nations to do the same. The idea of establishing a camp in North Africa was brought up at the Bermuda Conference but was later ignored. Once the Americans pledged to house refugees at Fort Ontario, the British seemed willing to do the same in North Africa. After Roosevelt announced his plans to bring refugees to Oswego, the British government responded by agreeing to establish a similar camp in Tripolitania, a former colony in North Africa with the capacity to house 1,500 people.[39] The plan stipulated that both Britain and the United States share the cost of maintaining the refugees. Unfortunately for the potential refugees, the British government procrastinated on the development of the camp and it never materialized.

The only North African camp that opened was at a former United States Army post in Fedala near Casablanca. The WRB supported the Fedala camp in the hope that it would receive refugees who had fled to Spain. Yet authorities in French North Africa blocked the establishment of the camp, citing security concerns.[40] Though the WRB promised to take responsibility for maintaining the refugees, the French feared that they would not leave after the war. As a result

---

38   Ibid., 289.
39   Text of a Telegram received by the Foreign Office on June 30: Text of message sent by the prime minister to the president, 30 June 1944; Papers of the War Refugee Board.
40   Wyman, *The Abandonment*, 260.

of French screening and procrastination, only 630 refugees arrived at Fedala in May of 1944.[41]

By establishing only a single camp within its borders, the United States failed to inspire the rest of the world to aid refugees. As Charles Joy of the Unitarian Service Committee remarked, "If the United States with all its resources can take only one thousand of these people what can we expect other countries to do?"[42] The War Refugee Board and the Roosevelt administration could expect other countries to do exactly what the United States did for refugees—less than was in their power.

---

41   Ibid., 261.
42   Ibid., 267.

CHAPTER THIRTEEN

Other Methods of Relief: The WRB and the Food Parcel Program

ANOTHER PROJECT THAT THE ALLIES opposed on the grounds that it would undermine the war effort was the sending of food parcels into concentration camps. The director of the WRB advocated for food parcel distribution. Shortly after the WRB's creation, Pehle said at a staff meeting, "We have long since passed the time [when we should have begun shipping food]. It no longer can, in any way, interfere with the war effort."[1] When Pehle made that statement, both Allied and Nazi policies stood in the way of food parcel distribution to concentration camps. On the one hand, the British and American blockade prevented the Allies from sending supplies into enemy territory except for prisoners of war. On the other hand, the Nazis refused to give prisoner of war status to Jews or political prisoners from countries controlled by Germany.

In an approach to the State Department, in February 1944, the World Jewish Congress (WJC) asked if the United States government would join the WJC's efforts to contribute funds so the Red Cross could buy and distribute food to the Jews in Europe. Assistant Secretary of State Breckinridge Long claimed that the United States government had limited resources but it would consult with Britain about financing specific projects through the Intergovernmental Committee on Refugees.[2] Long failed to consult the newly created War Refugee Board, perhaps fearing that its members would support

---

1 Wyman, *The Abandonment*, 283.
2 Memorandum: Remnant groups sponsored by World Jewish Congress, Visa Division, State Department, 23 February 1944; Papers of the War Refugee Board.

sending aid to those in enemy territory. Regardless the British refused to stop the blockade. The British Embassy professed sympathy for the Jews but stated its concern that the enemy might make money on the purchase of foodstuffs in enemy territory.[3] For the time being, neither the American nor British governments wished to place the lives of human beings before the possibility of the Axis' powers financial gain.

Though American and British government officials chose to limit their imaginations, private groups in the United States found ways to package food without sending money into enemy territory. Instead, foodstuffs came from neutral territories and were shipped to specific internees in concentration camps. Though these agencies obtained permission to send food through the blockade before the establishment of the WRB, the Board made the work of these groups easier by procuring licenses from the Treasury Department. For example, the WRB recommended that the American Jewish Joint Distribution Committee get a license to receive $12,000 per month to buy food packages in Switzerland.[4] The packages were later sent to internees in the Theresienstadt concentration camp. Under Pehle's direction, the JDC also received licenses for the purchase of supplies that might not reach their destinations. He agreed to the JDC's proposal to start a trial operation to get food to internees at a camp near Hanover, Germany.[5] Aware of the opposition he might encounter from other government departments such as State, Pehle often did not consult anyone outside the WRB or the Treasury about these transactions.

Although he helped private groups get supplies to concentration camps, Pehle still could not authorize large-scale food programs

---

3   Letter from British Embassy to the State Department, 29 February 1944; Papers of the War Refugee Board.

4   Memo to Liaison Officer, Foreign Funds Control from WRB. Subject: Purchase of food packages in Switzerland for internees in camps in Theresienstadt, 19 February 1944; Papers of the War Refugee Board.

5   WRB memorandum for the files signed by F. Hodel, 22 April 1944; Papers of the War Refugee Board.

unless the blockade was broken. With that goal in mind, War Refugee Board members, along with representatives from the State Department and the Foreign Economic Administration, met with the British secretary of economic warfare in July of 1944. The two countries agreed on an offer from the United States to send a total of 300,000 food parcels to enemy camps via the American Red Cross. As the WRB pointed out, "The amount of food which might fall into enemy hands could not affect the outcome of the war nor prolong it and the desperate situation of the people held in these camps makes it increasingly necessary to give them some assistance even though we may not have ironclad guarantees of 100 percent receipt by the intended beneficiaries."[6] Six months after stating the necessity of the food parcel situation, Pehle and other Board members finally convinced the blockade authorities to act.

Although the WRB managed to loosen the blockade only toward the end of the war, Pehle intended to take advantage of the little time he had left to get food into the hands of the victims of the Nazis. For example, since sugar was rationed throughout the United States during the war, Pehle personally wrote to the chief counsel of the Sugar Rationing Division to get permission for special coupons to accompany the sugar included in the food packages.[7] He emphasized the dire circumstances of the package recipients and the importance of getting food out immediately. Though Pehle did his best to move the food parcel program forward, months passed before the first parcels were sent. In addition to sugar, the WRB needed to purchase other supplies such as cheese, meat, powdered milk, and more from vendors, some of which already had large orders to fill from the United States Army. Other food items, such as biscuits, were unattainable and had to be substituted with something else. Instead of biscuits, the Board found a company willing to provide

---

6   Telegram to American Embassy in London from State Department, FEA, and WRB, 31 July 1944; Papers of the War Refugee Board.

7   Letter to Mr. Charles Quick, Chief Counsel Sugar Rationing Division from Pehle, 16 August 1944; Papers of the War Refugee Board.

dehydrated soup.[8] Despite the complex logistics involved, the Board sent out the majority of its proposed 300,000 food parcels in November to the International Committee of the Red Cross.[9] The ICRC stocked them in Sweden before sending them to the camps. The question remained, however, whether the intended recipients would receive the food.

The International Committee of the Red Cross put a few different methods in place to check whether the WRB food parcels reached the people for whom they were intended or whether they were stolen. After the Red Cross requested their cooperation, some concentration camp commanders allowed Red Cross representatives to visit the camps. While on site, the delegates ascertained that concentration camp inmates usually received the parcels. In fact the Red Cross reported that evidence of successful food parcel deliveries was strongest whenever their representatives visited a camp in person.[10] Whenever the Red Cross did not have permission to enter a concentration camp, return receipts were packed with the food. The plan was for the internee to send the receipt back to the Red Cross, thus proving that they received the package. In his examination of the food distribution program, Roswell McClelland reported to the WRB that a high number of receipt tags were returned from Bergen-Belsen and Dachau.[11] Because not all internees in concentration camps had permission to mail receipts, the lack of a receipt was less conclusive than the in-person Red Cross visits. Though imperfect, the food parcel program provided some aid to people in great need. McClelland mentioned that he met "a young Frenchman who escaped from the Flossenburg concentration camp and who stated that he literally would not have survived if it had not been for

---

8   Summary of availability of ingredients and packing materials needed for 300,000 relief parcels, no date; Papers of the War Refugee Board.

9   *Final Summary Report of the Executive Director, War Refugee Board,* 15 September 1945; Papers of the War Refugee Board.

10 Telegram to WRB from McClelland, 23 December 1944; Papers of the War Refugee Board.

11 Ibid.

the packages he received through ICRC."[12] As the food packed in America often reached camp inmates without incident, the program proved that even more lives could have been saved if the blockade authorities had cooperated with the WRB's food parcel plan earlier.

Although time was running out by the end of 1944 to save more lives, WRB members persisted in acquiring more food parcels. After shipping the initial 300,000 packages with help from the Red Cross, the WRB recommended that an additional 300,000 parcels be packed and sent to the camps in January of 1945.[13] At this stage of the war, finding vendors to provide food was only one of the many problems facing the WRB's food program. The longer the war went on, the more disorganized and unreliable rail transportation became in Germany. Disruptions in rail routes had the potential to literally derail the WRB's food program, since railways were used to transport food to camp inmates. One advantage to Germany's overall deterioration, however, was the change in attitude of the SS and other camp commanders. ICRC members had easier access to camps and met with less resistance than previously. McClelland described the commanders in multiple camps as being "unusually accommodating."[14] In Vienna a group of SS men in charge of the area's camps were "displaying all signs of willingness to collaborate certainly in any relief activities if not in more interesting work."[15] The "more interesting work" McClelland referred to was the possibility of evacuating Jews from the camps.

Before any rescue or relief operations could take place, however, the ICRC needed a means of transportation for food as well as humans. For the delivery of food parcels, McClelland suggested that the WRB send him money to procure trucks so the ICRC delegates

---

12 Ibid.

13 Draft of a memorandum for secretary of the treasury, chairman of the American National Red Cross, and executive director of the War Refugee Board, 20 January 1945; Papers of the War Refugee Board.

14 Telegram for WRB from McClelland, 22 January 1945; Papers of the War Refugee Board.

15 Ibid.

had a means of getting to the camps and delivering supplies.[16] Once again, time to send anything into German territory ran short, not only because of the impending conclusion of the war, but also because of a new Nazi tactic in regard to Jews. The Nazis no longer relied on gassing the Jews; instead, if the internees were no longer capable of work, the Nazis starved them to death. Still, as McClelland noted earlier, cracks existed in the camp system of command. During a meeting between the president of the ICRC and high-ranking SS officials, the SS officers indicated a willingness to "allow deliveries of all types by truck or other means of transport irrespective of nationality or race."[17] They also did not officially object to the idea of evacuations, though they refused to supply transportation for evacuees. In addition to cooperation from the Nazis, McClelland and the ICRC needed the Board to supply trucks.

At this critical point for the food program, the War Refugee Board underwent a significant change with the appointment of a new executive director. At Secretary of the Treasury Henry Morgenthau's request, Pehle left his post as head of the WRB to aid the Treasury as it disposed of extra war supplies. Army General William O'Dwyer took over Pehle's duties at the WRB in late January 1945. Although the second food parcel program went forward under his administration, O'Dwyer spent less time and energy on WRB matters than Pehle. The WRB still recognized the importance of sending a second shipment of food, medicine, and clothing "at once" to save the lives of starving Jews and other internees; however, it waited until late February to make that statement and still failed to act.[18] In the meantime McClelland waited for an answer to his request for transportation. He located some trucks in Switzerland, but the Swiss had little fuel and few tires. Finally, the Board asked the War Department to intervene. This time, the War Department

---

16   Ibid.
17   Telegram to secretary of state, Washington, from American Legation, Bern, 22 March 1945; Papers of the War Refugee Board.
18   Text of a memorandum of executive director of War Refugee Board unanimously approved at Board meeting, 20 February 1945; Papers of the War Refugee Board.

cooperated and authorized the provision of fuel from the United States Army stocks in France. Board representatives also went to France. While there, they arranged to supply tires for the trucks waiting in Switzerland.[19] Once the transportation was in place, the Red Cross started sending WRB parcels out to camps again.

As McClelland wrote in a letter to the WRB, the plan to send trucks into concentration camps met with small success.[20] McClelland and the ICRC rented only a few trucks at a time because of the expense involved. For example, in March of 1945 the ICRC rented six twelve-ton trucks to transport relief supplies to Buchenwald and helped a private Jewish organization rent four trucks bound for Bergen-Belsen.[21] Despite their ability to hold tons of food and supplies, the number of trucks was inadequate to carry supplies to meet the needs of tens of thousands of camp internees. Also, as more time passed, the packages might not arrive before the internees died or became malnourished. In February McClelland spoke with former Bergen-Belsen prisoners who had escaped to Switzerland. They told him that parcels reached the camp but that the number "was pitifully inadequate to need."[22] As land transport in German territory deteriorated further, the efforts of the WRB and the ICRC were less likely to succeed.

The food parcel program continued until April of 1945, with rented trucks transporting parcels to concentration camps at Dachau, Munich, Theresienstadt, and Mauthausen.[23] By this time, the WRB needed more food parcels. Its new director requested permission to send another 300,000 food packages into Europe. FDR rejected the proposal and told O'Dwyer that time constraints and the poor

---

19 *Final Summary Report of the Executive Director, War Refugee Board*, 15 September 1945; Papers of the War Refugee Board.

20 Telegram to WRB from McClelland, 23 March 1945; Papers of the War Refugee Board.

21 Ibid.

22 Telegram to WRB from McClelland, 2 February 1945; Papers of the War Refugee Board.

23 *Final Summary Report of the Executive Director, War Refugee Board*, 15 September 1945; Papers of the War Refugee Board.

transport infrastructure in German territory made another large-scale food parcel program impossible.[24] The president made valid points. The WRB no longer had months to find food vendors and packaging as the war was nearly over. In addition, the ICRC agreed with the president's assessment. It feared for the safety of ICRC personnel driving the relief trucks once the territory between Germany and Switzerland (the country from which parcels departed) was part of the war zone. Despite the validity of the president's argument in the spring of 1945, many more packages could have been sent if the WRB had permission from the government to start its food program earlier.

Though FDR and the circumstances of the war stopped the WRB's traditional method of delivering supplies to concentration camps, WRB members still sought more food parcels. Its leadership recognized that even when liberated, former inmates and inhabitants of countries dominated by Germany would still need food packages. The Board received permission from the War Department to purchase over 200,000 POW parcels.[25] In turn, the Board sold the parcels to the United Nations Relief and Rehabilitation Administration for delivery to displaced people in both Germany and other liberated areas.

It is impossible to know precisely how many concentration camp inmates received WRB food packages, or how many lives were saved as a result. As McClelland's encounter with the Flossenburg inmate indicated, however, the food parcel program played a role in keeping endangered people alive. In addition, the Red Cross rescued concentration camp refugees with the trucks acquired by McClelland. On return trips to Switzerland, the Red Cross brought out 1,400 refugees in April of 1945.[26]

---

24   Letter to William O'Dwyer, Executive Director War Refugee Board from Franklin
     Roosevelt, 5 April 1945; Papers of the War Refugee Board.
25   *Final Summary Report of the Executive Director, War Refugee Board*, 15 September 1945;
     Papers of the War Refugee Board.
26   Ibid.

CHAPTER FOURTEEN

Conclusions: An Evaluation of the WRB's Accomplishments

THE NUMBER OF JEWS AIDED by the War Refugee Board remains indefinite. Indeed, the numbers differ depending on which source the reader believes. In the *Final Summary Report* of the WRB, Executive Director William O'Dwyer stated that "tens of thousands" of people were physically rescued by the WRB. In addition the Board aided "hundreds of thousands" through relief programs such as the food parcels.[1] O'Dwyer's estimate is not only indefinite but refers vaguely to "people" helped by the WRB. He makes no distinction for the number of Jews who received assistance. As shown in Chapter Eight, the WRB successfully rescued groups of persecuted people, but not all of them were Jewish. In February 1945 the WRB released a somewhat more specific report in which it claimed to have rescued 126,604 people but did not mention the number of Jews.[2] In contrast to the reticence of the WRB, various historians credited the Board with saving many Jews. The most quoted estimate is 200,000. Historians David Wyman, Richard Breitman, and Rafael Medoff all cite the 200,000 figure in their Holocaust studies. Yet the WRB never claimed it rescued 200,000 people, much less 200,000 Jewish refugees.

---

1   *Final Summary Report of the Executive Director, War Refugee Board*, 15 September 1945; Papers of the War Refugee Board.
2   War Refugee Board inter-office communication to the executive director from P. J. McCormack Re: Number of Persons Rescued since the Establishment of the War Refugee Board, 19 February 1945; Papers of the War Refugee Board.

Another problem with arriving at a specific number is that some aspects of the WRB's work are difficult to quantify. The Board's representative in Turkey, Ira Hirschmann, cited the renewed hope of the refugees as one of the Board's accomplishments. He said the WRB's creation "injected new life and hope into ... refugees throughout the European continent."[3] No one will ever be able to measure the hope engendered in the Jews of Europe by the United States' new commitment to rescue them.

Taking into account the direct rescues performed by the WRB's representatives and the Red Cross, whose cooperation with rescues the WRB secured at the end of the war, this author arrived at an estimate of 130,000 rescued Jews. That number includes only Jews who were physically saved by the WRB's efforts, however. The Board's methods of psychological warfare, funding of underground rescue groups, and its commitment to sending food and supplies to Jews in the camps and the Budapest ghetto undoubtedly helped thousands of others to survive. In addition, as mentioned earlier, the WRB also saved thousands of non-Jewish refugees. The 200,000 estimate arrived at by Wyman and others may be feasible if applied to the total number of people saved by the WRB, though not the number of Jews alone.

Though no one agrees on how many Jews the Board helped, historians as well as former Board members concur that more people, including Jews, could have been saved if the WRB existed prior to January 1944. The Board's longest serving director, John Pehle, said, "What we [the Board members] did was little enough. It was late ... late and little I would say."[4] Other members agreed that the WRB's accomplishments were impeded by its late start on rescue and relief attempts. After the Board's termination, Ira Hirschmann said, "It is regrettable that the Board, which has demonstrated its vitality and the success of its operations, was not created a year or two ago. There is no doubt from the evidence at hand that additional thousands of refugees could have been saved."[5] The War Refugee Board encountered many

---

3   Wyman, *The Abandonment*, 221.
4   Ibid., 287.
5   Morse, 382–3.

failures and limitations, and these sometimes outweighed its successes.

Most historians, like the former Board members, focus on what the WRB failed to accomplish. Granted, the Board could have saved more lives if FDR had created it sooner; however, it did do some good. In Hungary, for example, an estimated 250,000 out of almost one million Jews survived the war.[6] The statistics look unimpressive at first glance, but without the efforts of the WRB and Raoul Wallenberg, the Nazis could easily have wiped out Hungary's entire Jewish population. The Board deserves commendation for what it achieved during 1944 and early 1945. Its accomplishments included gaining time; rescuing some Jews via negotiations with Nazis and Axis government officials; stopping Hungarian deportations with psychological warfare; opening travel routes; saving Budapest's remaining Jews; establishing a food parcel program and the Oswego refugee camp. The War Refugee Board served as America's belated conscience by providing during its brief existence more aid to the Jews of the Holocaust than the United States offered prior to the Board's creation. Indeed, considering the roadblocks the Board encountered from the Nazis, the British, and even members of the United States government, the rescue of any refugees remains a testament to the dedication of the Board's members, who pushed and prodded to save lives by various means.

Although the Board's accomplishments in the field of rescue and relief were nothing short of amazing, its greatest achievement lay in redefining war crimes. The United Nations Commission on War Crimes was created in 1943. When the WRB came into existence, Director John Pehle often used the threat of future punishment to encourage the Nazis to stop persecuting Jews and other minorities. Therefore, members of the Board reacted with shock when they learned that many crimes against Jews might not be punished at all. Herbert Pell, the American representative at the UN Commission, informed the Board that the Commission's

6   War Refugee Board inter-office communication to the executive director from P.J.
      McCormack Re: Number of Persons Rescued since the Establishment of the War
      Refugee Board, 19 February 1945; Papers of the War Refugee Board.

definition of war crimes did not include acts committed by Nazis or their satellites against Jews who resided in Axis territory. Instead, the Commission's definition of war crimes included only crimes by one warring nation against another.[7] When Pell wrote to WRB member Josiah DuBois and gave him this information, DuBois balked at the limitations of the definition. Both he and Pell agreed that the Nazis should be punished for all war atrocities, but Pell needed the WRB's backing.[8] He got it when DuBois shared Pell's dilemma with Pehle. Incensed by DuBois' news, Pehle wrote an emphatic letter to the State Department requesting that State inform Pell that the policy of the United States government was to pursue all war criminals regardless of the location or nationality of their victims. Pehle wrote, "It would be a fearful miscarriage of justice if such war criminals were permitted to escape punishment for their inhumane crimes. Moreover, the failure to implement the numerous threats of punishment ... would render it far more difficult to deter similar criminal conduct in the future."[9] Pehle was thinking not only of Nazi atrocities, but also about war crimes that others might commit in the future.

As they had so many times when the WRB called upon them to act on behalf of persecuted minorities, the State Department did nothing in response to Pehle's letter. Three months later the department claimed that the war crimes issue was still "under consideration."[10] In fact State's objective was to block the passage of a broader definition of war crimes. By December 1944, Pell returned to Washington, since he had received no instructions from State on how to proceed at the War Crimes Commission. Knowing that Pell was sympathetic to the Jews, State Department members insisted

---

7   Letter to John Pehle from James Mann, American Embassy London, 19 September 1944; Papers of the War Refugee Board.

8   Josiah DuBois, memorandum for the files, 17 August 1944; Morgenthau Diaries, 805/8–9, 11–14, 16–17; FDR Library, Hyde Park, NY.

9   John Pehle, memorandum for Mr. Stettinius, 28 August 1944; Morgenthau Diaries, 805/8–9, 11–14, 16–17; FDR Library, Hyde Park, NY.

10 Memo on Jurisdiction of War Crimes Commission over Murder of Jews, 23 December 1944; quoted in Rafael Medoff, *Blowing the Whistle on Genocide*, 109.

that Pell could not return to the Commission's meeting in London because Congress had failed to provide the money for his trip. State did, however, manage to help the War Department find and pay for Pell's replacement.[11]

By now both State and Pell himself believed that the cause of punishing all Nazi war criminals was dead. Yet they forgot one important point mentioned in John Pehle's original letter to the State Department. In addition to suggesting that the department offer support to Herbert Pell's cause, Pehle wrote that another possible step would be to publicize State support in the press.[12] Of course State gave no such instruction, but the press could still be utilized to help spread the word that war criminals were going unpunished. The accounts of two Jews who had escaped from Auschwitz and Birkenau had already been released to the press thanks to Pehle's insistence. Public reaction to the reports reflected almost unanimous shock.

Peter Bergson, who successfully publicized so many other accounts of Nazi persecution during the Holocaust, heard about Pell's predicament through "friendly sources."[13] Only the State Department and the War Refugee Board knew about State's attempts to block Pell's reappointment to the United Nations War Crimes Commission. Bergson always lamented the Board's limited authority, but he respected some of its individual members. He referred to John Pehle as a "good guy" and stayed in contact with him and DuBois after FDR created the Board.[14] Bergson did not feel the same way about the State Department, and it is unlikely that State would reveal its opposition to a tougher war crimes definition to the head of the Emergency Committee to Save the Jewish People of Europe.

---

11   Memo by Herbert Pell, July 1945; quoted in Rafael Medoff, *Blowing the Whistle on Genocide*, 110.

12   John Pehle, memorandum for Mr. Stettinius, 28 August 1944; Morgenthau Diaries, 805/8–9, 11–14, 16–17; FDR Library, Hyde Park, NY.

13   Memo by Samuel Merlin, leader of the Bergson Group, February 1945; quoted in Rafael Medoff, *Blowing the Whistle on Genocide*, 111.

14   Wyman, *A Race Against Death*, 163.

His friendly source of information must have been a member of the WRB. Armed with the knowledge of State's duplicity, Bergson convinced a devastated Pell to tell his story to the press. One of Bergson's colleagues wrote, "We organized this press conference and forced the issue into the open. Mr. Pell made a remarkably forceful statement that won front-page prominence in New York and Washington papers. It put the State Department on the defensive and forced both Secretary Stettinius and Undersecretary Grew to issue statements indicating that our Government would insist on the punishment of those guilty of crimes against the Hebrew people."[15] Thanks to the efforts of Pehle, DuBois, and Bergson, the War Crimes Commission broadened the definition of war crimes, meaning not only that many Nazi perpetrators could be brought to justice but also forever changing the United States' position on war crimes.

The immediate effect of the WRB's insistence on a broader war crimes definition occurred at the trial of Nazi leaders at an international court in Nuremberg, Germany. For the first time, the prosecution sought to indict on charges of both war crimes and crimes against humanity. At Nuremberg all war crimes became crimes against humanity, though the reverse was not always true. For example, acts committed on enemy occupied territory might be war crimes and crimes against humanity, but crimes against humanity could occur whether or not a state of war existed.[16] War crimes were forever connected to the United Nations' concept of crimes against humanity. Article Six of the Nuremberg Charter stated that the following acts were among the "crimes coming within the jurisdiction of the Tribunal for which there shall be individual responsibility ... Crimes against humanity, namely, murder, extermination, enslavement, deportation, and other inhumane acts committed against any civilian population, before or during the war, or persecutions on political, racial or religious grounds ... whether or not in violation of the domestic law of the country where

---

15   Ibid.
16   The United Nations War Crimes Commission, *History of the United Nations War Crimes Commission and the Laws of War* (London: His Majesty's Stationary Office, 1948), 188.

perpetrated."[17] The WRB was the first government agency in the world to support punishment for crimes committed by a nation against its own citizens. As a result WRB members were indirectly responsible for the inclusion of crimes against humanity as a charge at Nuremberg.

Before the trial began, Hitler committed suicide, but the international court put twenty-one major German war criminals on trial. Seventeen of those were charged with crimes against humanity. Only two were found not guilty of the charge. The others were sentenced to hanging or imprisonment.[18] After the main trial, the United States independently conducted twelve other trials that involved the indictment of lesser-known Nazi operatives such as doctors and SS officers. The fact that the United States unilaterally decided to try these Nazis is ironic when one considers that the State Department initially had no intention of holding former Nazis accountable for their actions.

The definition of crimes against humanity established at Nuremberg remained a principle of United States foreign policy long after the Nazi trials. In the 1990s, Serbian leader Slobodan Milošević and his henchmen in the Balkans killed thousands of Albanians and Croatians. The genocide was conducted with the goal of "ethnic cleansing," reminiscent of Hitler's goal to exterminate the Jews of Europe and leave only members of the Aryan race alive. Though some of Milošević's helpers went to trial earlier, his trial began in 2002 and lasted four years. The Milošević trial raised the crimes against humanity statute to a new level, since Milošević was the first head of state who faced criminal charges before an international court. Milošević died in his cell before the prosecution could sentence him. However, others who worked with him on the ethnic-cleansing program were sent to prison for their actions.[19]

An ethnic majority in Rwanda also committed crimes against

---

17   Ibid., 191.
18   Norbert Ehrenfreund, *The Nuremberg Legacy* (New York: Palgrave Macmillan, 2007), 87.
19   Ibid., 156–7.

humanity in the 1990s. A conflict between two Rwandan tribes, the Hutu and the Tutsi, led to the killing of 800,000 people in 1994. In addition to crimes against humanity, the Rwandan court added a definition of genocide. The court defined genocide as acts committed with the intent to destroy, in whole or in part, a national, ethnic, racial, or religious group. In September of 1998 former Rwandan Prime Minister Jean Kambanda received a life sentence for genocide. Other military leaders who carried out the killings were also sentenced to life in prison.[20]

The support of a broader war crimes definition stands as the War Refugee Board's most enduring accomplishment. However, one could argue that it is more reactive than proactive to charge people with war crimes after they commit them rather than intervening while the crimes are being committed.

As Eleanor Roosevelt said in reference to the Holocaust: "When will our consciences grow so tender that we will act to prevent human misery rather than avenge it?"[21] The answer is when people like the men and women of the War Refugee Board receive the time, money, and resources to do what their consciences tell them to do.

---

20   Ibid. 159–160.
21   Blanche Wiesen Cook, *Eleanor Roosevelt, Volume One 1884–1933* (New York: Penguin
      Books, 1992), 17.

APPENDIX 1

Personal Report to the President

ONE OF THE GREATEST CRIMES in history, the slaughter of the Jewish people in Europe, is continuing unabated.

This government has for a long time maintained that its policy is to work out programs to save those Jews and other persecuted minorities of Europe who could be saved.

You are probably not as familiar as I with the utter failure of certain officials in our State Department, who are charged with actually carrying out this policy, to take any effective action to prevent the extermination of the Jews in German-controlled Europe.

The public record, let alone the facts which have not yet been made public, reveals the gross procrastination of these officials. It is well known that since the time when it became clear that Hitler was determined to carry out a policy of exterminating the Jews in Europe, the State Department officials have failed to take any positive steps reasonably calculated to save any of these people. Although they have used devices such as setting up intergovernmental organizations to survey the whole refugee problem, and calling conferences such as the Bermuda Conference to explore the whole refugee problem, making it appear that positive action could be expected, in fact nothing has been accomplished.

The best summary of the whole situation is contained in one sentence of a report submitted on December 20, 1943, by the Committee on Foreign Relations of the Senate, recommending the passage of a Resolution (S.R. 203), favoring the appointment of a commission to formulate plans to save the Jews of Europe from extinction by Nazi Germany. The Resolution had been introduced by Senator Guy M. Gillette in [*sic*] behalf of himself and eleven colleagues, Senators Taft, Thomas, Radcliffe, Murray, Johnson, Guffey, Ferguson, Clark, Van Nuys, Downey and Ellender. The Committee stated:

"We have talked, we have sympathized; we have expressed our horror; the time to act is long past due."

Whether one views this failure as being deliberate on the part of those officials handling the matter, or merely due to their incompetence, is not too important from my point of view. However, there is a growing number of responsible people and organizations today who have ceased to view our failure as the product of simple incompetence on the part of those officials in the State Department charged with handling this problem. They see plain Anti-Semitism motivating the actions of these State Department officials and, rightly or wrongly, it will require little more in the way of proof for this suspicion to explode into a nasty scandal.

In this perspective, I ask you to weigh the implications of the following two cases which have recently come to my attention and which have not as yet become known to the public.

I.

World Jewish Congress Proposal to Evacuate Thousands of Jews from Rumania and France

On March 13, 1943, the World Jewish Congress representative in London sent a cable to their offices here. This cable stated that information reaching London indicated it was possible to rescue Jews provided funds were put at the disposal of the World Jewish Congress representation in Switzerland.

On April 10, 1943, Sumner Welles cabled our Legation in Bern and requested them to get in touch with the World Jewish Congress representative in Switzerland, who Welles had been informed was in possession of important information regarding the Jews.

On April 20, 1943, the State Department received a cable from Bern relating to the proposed financial arrangements in connection with the evacuation of the Jews from Rumania and France.

On May 25, 1943, State Department cabled for a clarification of these proposed financial arrangements. This matter was not called to the attention of the Treasury Department at this time although the Treasury has the responsibility for licensing all such financial transactions.

This whole question of financing the evacuation of the Jews from Rumania and France was first called to the attention of the Treasury Department on June 25, 1943.

A conference was held with the State Department relating to this matter on July 15, 1943.

One day after this conference, on July 16, 1943, the Treasury Department advised the State Department that it was prepared to issue a license in this matter.

It was not until December 18, 1943, after having interposed objections for five months, that the State Department, precipitously and under circumstances revealing the fictitious character of their objections, instructed Harrison to issue the necessary license.

During this five months period between the time that the Treasury stated that it was prepared to issue a license and the time when the license was actually issued delays and objections of all sorts were forthcoming from officials in the State Department, our Legation in Bern, and finally the British. The real significance of these delays and objections was brought home to the State Department in letters which I sent to Secretary Hull on November 23, 1943, and December 17, 1943, which completely devastated the excuses which State

Department officials had been advancing.

On December 18 I made an appointment to discuss the matter with Secretary Hull on December 20. And then an amazing but understandable thing happened. On the very day I made my appointment the State Department issued a license notwithstanding the fact that the objections of our Legation in Bern were still outstanding and that the British had indicated their disapproval for political reasons.

State Department officials were in such a hurry to issue this license that they not only did not ask the Treasury to draft the license (which would have been the normal procedure) but they drafted the license themselves and issued it without even consulting the Treasury as to its terms. Informal discussions with certain State Department officials have confirmed what is obvious from the above-mentioned facts.

This wasn't all that my letter and appointment precipitated. I had told Secretary Hull that I wished to discuss the British objections – in simple terms, the British were apparently prepared to accept the probable death of thousands of Jews in enemy territory because of "the difficulties of disposing of any considerable number of Jews should they be rescued." Accordingly, on that day of "action" for our State Department, December 18, they sent a telegram expressing astonishment with the British point of view and stating that the Department was unable to agree with that point of view.

Breckinridge Long, who is in charge of such matters in the State Department, knew that his position was so indefensible that he was unwilling even to try to defend it at my pending conference with Secretary Hull on December 20. Accordingly, he took such action as he felt was necessary to cover up his previous position in this matter. It is, of course, clear that if we had not made the record against the State Department followed by my request to see Secretary Hull, the action which the State Department officials took on December 18 would either never have been taken at all or would have been delayed so long that any benefits which it might have had would have been lost.

II.

Suppression of Facts Regarding Hitler's Extermination of Jews in Europe

The facts are as follows:

Sumner Welles as Acting Secretary of State requests confirmation of Hitler's plan to exterminate the Jews. Having already received various reports on the plight of the Jews, on October 5, 1942 Sumner Welles as Acting Secretary of State sent a cable (2314) for the personal attention of Minister Harrison in Bern stating that leaders of the Jewish Congress had received reports from their representatives in Geneva and London to the effect that many thousands of Jews in Eastern Europe were being slaughtered pursuant to a policy embarked on by the German Government for the complete extermination of the Jews in Europe. Welles added that he was trying to obtain further information from the Vatican but that other than this he was unable to secure confirmation of these stories. He stated that Rabbi Wise believed that information was available to his representatives in Switzerland but that they were in all likelihood fearful of dispatching any such reports through open cables or mail. He then stated that World Jewish Congress officials in Switzerland, Riegner and Lichtheim, were being requested by Wise to call upon Minister Harrison; and Welles requested Minister Harrison to advise him by telegram of all the evidence and facts which he might secure as a result of conferences with Riegner and Lichtheim.

State Department receives confirmation that the extermination was being rapidly carried out. Pursuant to Welles' cable of October 5 Minister Harrison forwarded documents from Riegner confirming the fact of extermination of the Jews (in November 1942), and in a cable of January 21, 1943 (482) relayed a message from Riegner and Lichtheim which Harrison stated was for the information of the Under Secretary of State (and was to be transmitted to Rabbi Stephen Wise if the Under Secretary should so determine). This message described a horrible situation concerning the plight of Jews in Europe. It reported mass executions of Jews in Poland; the Jews were required before execution to strip themselves of all their clothing which was then sent to Germany; in Germany deportations were continuing; many Jews were being deprived of rationed foodstuffs; no Jews would be left in Prague or Berlin by the end of March, etc; and in Rumania 130,000 Jews were deported to Transnistria; about 60,000 had already died and the remaining 70,000 were starving; living conditions were indescribable; Jews were deprived of all their money, foodstuffs and possessions; they were housed in deserted cellars, and occasionally twenty to thirty people slept on the floor of one unheated room; disease was prevalent, particularly fever; urgent assistance was needed.

Sumner Welles furnishes this information to the Jewish organizations. Sumner Welles furnished the documents received in November to the Jewish organizations in the United States and authorized them to make the facts public. On February 9, 1943 Welles forwarded the messages contained in cable 482 of January 21 to Rabbi Stephen Wise.

The receipt of this message intensified the pressure on the State Department to take some action.

Certain State Department officials attempt to stop this Government from obtaining further information from the very source from which the above evidence was received. On February 10, the day after Welles forwarded the message contained in cable 482 of January 21 to Rabbi Wise, and in direct response to this cable, a most highly significant cable was dispatched to Minister Harrison. This cable, 354 of February 10, read as follows:

"Your 482, January 21

"In the future we would suggest that you do not accept reports submitted to you to be transmitted to private persons in the United States unless such action is advisable because of extraordinary circumstances. Such private messages circumvent neutral countries' censorship and it is felt that by sending them we risk the possibility that steps would necessarily be taken by the neutral countries to curtail or forbid our means of communication for confidential official matter[s].

Hull (SW)"

The cable was signed for Hull by "SW" (Sumner Welles). But it is significant that there is not a word in it that would even suggest to the person signing it that it was designed to countermand the Department's specific requests for information on Hitler's plans to exterminate the Jews. The cable has the appearance of being a normal routine message which a busy official would sign without question. On its face it is most innocent and innocuous, yet when read together with the previous cables is it anything less than an attempted suppression of information requested by this Government concerning the murder of the Jews by Hitler?

It is also significant that the message which provoked the ban on further communications of this character was not addressed to private persons at all but was addressed to Under Secretary Welles at his own request and the information contained therein was only to be transmitted to the World Jewish Congress if Welles deemed it advisable.

Thereafter on April 10, 1943, Sumner Welles again requested our Legation for information (cable 877). Apparently he did not realize that in cable 354 (to which he did not refer) Harrison had been instructed to cease forwarding reports of this character. Harrison replied on April 20 (cable 2460) and indicated that he was in a most confused state of mind as a result of the conflicting instructions he had received. Among other things he stated:

"May I suggest that messages of this character should not (repeat not) be subjected to the restriction imposed by your 354, February 10, and that I be permitted to transmit messages from R more particularly in view of the helpful information which they may frequently contain?"

The fact that cable 354 is not the innocent and routine cable that it appears to be on its face is further highlighted by the efforts of State Department officials to prevent this Department from obtaining the cable and learning its true significance.

The facts relating to this attempted concealment are as follows:

i.   Several men in our Department had requested State Department officials for a copy of the cable of February 10 (354). We had been advised that it was a Department communication; a strictly political communication, which had nothing to do with economic matters; that it had only had a very limited distribution within the Department, the only ones having anything to do with it being the European Division, the Political Advisor and Sumner Welles; and that a copy could not be furnished to the Treasury.

ii.   At the conference in Secretary Hull's office on December 20 in the presence of Breckinridge Long I asked Secretary Hull for a copy of cable 354, which I was told would be furnished to me.

iii.   By note to me of December 20, Breckinridge Long enclosed a paraphrase of cable 354. This paraphrase of cable 354 specifically omitted any reference to cable 482 of January 21 – thus destroying the only tangible clue to the true meaning of the message.

iv.   I would never have learned the true meaning of cable 354 had it not been for chance. I had asked one of the men in my Department to obtain all the facts on this matter. He had previously called one of the men in another Division of the State Department and requested permission to see the relevant cables. In view of the Treasury interest in this matter, this State Department representative obtained cable 354 and the cable of January 21 to which it referred and showed these cables to my representative.

The facts I have detailed in this report, Mr. President, came to the Treasury's attention as a part of our routine investigation of the licensing of the financial phases of the proposal of the World Jewish Congress for the evacuation of Jews from France and Rumania. The facts may thus be said to have come to light through accident. How many others of the same character are buried in State Department files is a matter I would have no way of knowing. Judging from the almost complete failure of the State Department to achieve any results, the strong suspicion must be that they are not few.

This much is certain, however. The matter of rescuing the Jews from extermination is a trust too great to remain in the hands of men who are indifferent, callous, and perhaps even hostile. The task is filled with difficulties. Only a fervent will to accomplish, backed by persistent and untiring effort can succeed where time is so precious.

Henry Morgenthau
Jan. 16, 1944.

Executive Order No. 9417
Establishing a War Refugee Board

WHEREAS IT IS THE POLICY of this Government to take all measures within its power to rescue the victims of enemy oppression who are in imminent danger of death and otherwise to afford such victims all possible relief and assistance consistent with the successful prosecution of the war:

Now, therefore, by the virtue of the authority vested in me by the Constitution and the statutes of the United States, as President of the United States and Commander in Chief of the Army and Navy, and in order to effectuate with all possible speed the rescue and relief of such victims of enemy oppression, it is hereby ordered as follows:

1   There is established in the Executive Office of the President a War Refugee Board (hereinafter referred to as the Board). The Board shall consist of the Secretary of State, the Secretary of the Treasury and the Secretary of War. The Board may request the heads of other agencies or departments to participate in its deliberations whenever matters specifically affecting such agencies or departments are under consideration.

2   The Board shall be charged with the responsibility for seeing that the policy of the Government, as stated in the Preamble, is carried out. The functions of the Board shall include without limitation the development of plans and programs and the inauguration of effective measures for (a) the rescue, transportation, maintenance and relief

of the victims of enemy oppression, and (b) the establishment of havens of temporary refuge for such victims. To this end the Board, through appropriate channels, shall take the necessary steps to enlist the cooperation of foreign governments and obtain their participation in the execution of such plans and programs.

3   It shall be the duty of the State, Treasury and War Departments, within their respective spheres, to execute at the request of the Board, the plans and programs so developed and the measures so inaugurated. It shall be the duty of the heads of all agencies and departments to supply or obtain for the Board such information and to extend to the Board such supplies, shipping and other specified assistance and facilities as the Board may require in carrying out the provisions of this Order. The State Department shall appoint special attaches with diplomatic status, on the recommendation of the Board, to be stationed abroad in places where it is likely that assistance can be rendered to war refugees, the duties and responsibilities of such attaches to be defined by the Board in consultation with the State Department.

4   The Board and the State, Treasury and War Departments are authorized to accept the services or contributions of any private persons, private organizations, State agencies, or agencies of foreign governments in carrying out the purposes of this Order. The Board shall cooperate with all existing and future international organizations concerned with the problems of refugee rescue, maintenance, transportation, relief, rehabilitation, and resettlement.

5   To the extent possible the Board shall utilize the personnel, supplies, facilities and services of the State, Treasury and War Departments. In addition the Board, within the limits of funds which may be made available, may employ necessary personnel without regard for the Civil Service laws and regulations and the Classification Act of 1923, as amended, and make provisions for supplies, facilities and services necessary to discharge its responsibilities. The Board shall appoint an Executive Director who shall serve as its principal executive officer. It shall be the duty of the Executive Director to arrange for the prompt execution of the plans and programs developed and the measures

inaugurated by the Board, to supervise the activities of the special attaches and to submit frequent reports to the Board on the steps taken for the rescue and relief of war refugees.

6   The Board shall be directly responsible to the President in carrying out the policy of this Government, as stated in the Preamble, and the Board shall report to him at frequent intervals concerning the steps taken for the rescue and relief of war refugees and shall make such recommendations as the Board may deem appropriate for further action to overcome any difficulties encountered in the rescue and relief of war refugees.

Franklin D. Roosevelt
The White House
January 22, 1944

Memorandum for Mr. Stettinius

As you know, a major activity of the War Refugee Board has been psychological warfare designed to induce and persuade the enemy to cease the persecution of the Jews and other minorities. The basis of this program, which has been carried out in cooperation with the State Department, Office of War Information and other agencies, has been the threat to punish every Axis war criminal who has participated, directly or indirectly, in such persecution. Threats of this nature had been made by the United Nations, including various branches of this Government, even before the War Refugee Board was established, and they have since been repeated with increasing tempo. For your information we have collected and are attaching hereto those declarations which specifically set forth the determination of the United States and of other United Nations to punish the perpetrators of atrocities and other crimes against Jews and other minorities even where the victims are or were nationals of Germany or of a satellite power.

We had assumed that one of the primary functions of the United Nations Commission for the Investigation of War Crimes which was created in 1943, would be to devise procedures for the gathering of evidence and the ascertainment, trial and punishment of those enemy nationals who had participated in such war crimes. Much to our surprise we were informed by our General Counsel, Mr. Josiah E. DuBois, upon his return from London recently that he understood from a conversation with Mr. Pell, the United States representative on the Commission, that the Commission takes the view that war crimes under international law do not include crimes committed by an Axis nation or its nationals against its own subjects or the subjects of another Axis nation. Accordingly, it appears that the Commission is not making any provision for the just punishment for such war criminals.

Needless to say, it would be a fearful miscarriage of justice if such war criminals were permitted to escape punishment for their inhuman crimes. Moreover, the failure to implement the numerous threats of punishment would not only subject to ridicule the authors thereof, but would render it far more difficult to deter similar criminal conduct in the future. The failure to punish the criminals of World War I may well have removed a deterrent to the commission of brutalities against civilian populations in this war, including the mass murder of the Jews.

According to Mr. DuBois' report, Mr. Pell is not satisfied with this position of the United Nations Commission for the Investigation of War Crimes, but seems not to have received instructions from this Government in the matter. Mr. Pell believes that the most effective way of inducing the Commission to broaden the scope of its work to include the punishment of all Axis war criminals, including those guilty of crimes against persons in the above categories, would be to have the United States Government instruct him to urge the Commission to include such crimes in its program and, if possible, to have the other governments represented on the Commission instruct their representatives along similar lines. Another suggested step would be to publicize such an instruction by releasing it to the press.

Accordingly, we suggest that the Department advise Mr. Pell along the lines of the proposed cable attached hereto indicating clearly that the declared policy of the United States Government is to ensure the just punishment of all Axis war criminals, including those guilty of crimes against the Jews and other minorities whether or not the victims of such crimes are of the same nationality as the evildoers; and that Mr. Pell should insist upon the formulation of a program by the Commission effectuating this policy.

(Signed) J. W. Pehle
Executive Director
August 28, 1944

Cable from the Department to Ambassador Winant For H. C. Pell, London, England

IN CONNECTION WITH MR. PELL'S work on the United Nations Commission for the Investigation of War Crimes he should be advised of the following:

A joint statement was issued on December 17, 1942 by the Governments of the United States, Belgium, Czechoslovakia, Greece, Luxembourg, Norway, Poland, Russia, United Kingdom and Yugoslavia and the French National Committee condemning the brutal slaughter of the Jews of Europe by the Germans. The statement concludes:

QUOTE

The above-mentioned Governments and the French National Committee condemn in the strongest possible terms this bestial policy of cold-blooded extermination. They declare that such events can only strengthen the resolve of all freedom-loving peoples to overthrow the barbarous Hitlerite tyranny. They reaffirm their solemn resolution to insure that those responsible for these crimes shall not escape retribution and to press on with the necessary practical measures to this end.

END QUOTE

The United States Congress in March 1943 passed a concurrent resolution, which after reciting the atrocities afflicted on the Jews by the Nazis, resolved as follows:

QUOTE

That these brutal and indefensible outrages against millions of helpless men, women, and children should be, and they are hereby, condemned as unworthy of any nation or in any regime which pretends to be civilized:

RESOLVED FURTHER, That the dictates of humanity and honorable conduct in war demand that this inexcusable slaughter and mistreatment shall cease and that it is the sense of the Congress that those guilty, directly or indirectly, of these criminal acts shall be held accountable and punished in a manner commensurate with the offenses for which they are responsible.

END QUOTE

On March 24, 1944, President Roosevelt issued a statement condemning the systematic torture and murder of civilians by the Nazis and of civilians and American soldiers by the Japanese. He also made the following specific reference to the slaughter of the Jews and the punishment by the United Nations of those who participated therein:

QUOTE

In one of the blackest crimes of all history – begun by the
Nazis in the day of peace and multiplied by them a hundred
times in time of war – the wholesale systematic murder of
the Jews of Europe goes on unabated every hour. As a result
of the events of the last few days hundreds of thousands of
Jews, who while living under persecution have at least found
a haven from death in Hungary and the Balkans, are now
threatened with annihilation as Hitler's forces descend more
heavily upon these lands. That these innocent people, who
have already survived a decade of Hitler's fury, should perish
on the very eve of triumph over the barbarism which their
persecution symbolizes, would be a major tragedy.

It is therefore fitting that we should again proclaim our
determination that none who participate in these acts of
savagery shall go unpunished. The United Nations have made
it clear that they will pursue the guilty and deliver them up
in order that justice be done. That warning applies not only
to the leaders but also to their functionaries and subordinates
in Germany and in the satellite countries. All who knowingly
take part in the deportation of Jews to their death in Poland
or Norwegians and French to their death in Germany are
equally guilty with the executioner. All who share the guilt
shall share the punishment.

END QUOTE

On March 30, 1944 Anthony Eden stated on the floor of the
House of Commons that His Majesty's Government wholeheartedly
concurred in the above views of President Roosevelt. He said further

QUOTE

Evidence continues to reach His Majesty's Government and Allied Governments that the Nazi policy of extermination has not been halted. The persecution of the Jews has in particular been of unexampled horror and intensity. On this His Majesty's Government in common with their Allies, now that the hour of Germany's defeat grows ever nearer and more certain, can only repeat their detestation of Germany's crimes and their determination that all those guilty of them shall be brought to Justice. But apart from direct guilt there is still indirect participation in crime. Satellite governments who expel citizens to destinations named by Berlin must know that such actions are tantamount to assisting in inhuman persecution or slaughter. This will not be forgotten when the inevitable defeat of the arch enemy of Europe comes about.

END QUOTE

Secretary Hull on July 15, 1944, addressing himself specifically to the brutal persecution of Jews in Hungary, said:

QUOTE

Reliable reports from Hungary have confirmed the appalling news of mass killing of Jews by the Nazis and their Hungarian quislings. The number of victims of these fiendish crimes is great. The entire Jewish community in Hungary, which numbered one million souls, is threatened with extermination. The horror and indignation felt by the American people at these coldblooded tortures and massacres has been voiced by the President, by the Congress, and by hundreds of private organizations throughout the country. It is shared by all civilized nations of the world. This government will not slacken its efforts to rescue as many of these unfortunate people as can be saved from persecution and death.

The puppet Hungarian government, by its violation of the most elementary human rights and by its servile adoption of the worst features of the Nazi 'racial policy', stands condemned before history. It may be futile to appeal to the humanity of the instigators or perpetrators of such outrages. Let them know that they cannot escape the inexorable punishment which will be meted out to them when the power of the evil men now in control of Hungary has been broken.

END QUOTE

The foregoing emphatically declares the policy of the United States, as well as of other United Nations, to see to it that all Axis nationals guilty of war crimes, including those against Jews and other minorities whether or not the victims were of the same nationality as the criminals, shall be ascertained, tried and punished.

Please advise whether the United Nations Commission to Investigate War Crimes has devised a program and procedures to effectuate the foregoing policy with respect to war crimes against the above-mentioned groups. If no such program and procedures have as yet been formulated, you are instructed to inform the Commission of this Government's policy with regard thereto and of its dissatisfaction with any program adopted by the Commission that will not take into account the punishment of Axis war criminals for crimes against Jews and other minorities whether or not they are nationals of enemy countries.

BIBLIOGRAPHY

Archival Sources

Diaries of Henry Morgenthau, Jr. Franklin D. Roosevelt Library, Hyde Park, NY.

Lester, Robert, comp. *Papers of the War Refugee Board.* Franklin D. Roosevelt Library, Hyde Park, NY; Bethesda, MD: UPA Collection from LexisNexis, 2002. Pennsylvania State University. Microfilm.

Papers of the War Refugee Board. Franklin D. Roosevelt Library, Hyde Park, NY.

Other Primary Sources

Abzug, Robert, ed. *America Views the Holocaust 1933–1945: A Brief Documentary History.* Boston: Bedford/St. Martin's, 1999.

Blum, John Morton, ed. *From the Morgenthau Diaries: Years of War 1941–1945.* Boston: Houghton Mifflin Co., 1967.

Collins, Ross F. *World War I: Primary Documents on Events from 1914–19.* West Port, CT: Greenwood Press, 2008.

Gruber, Ruth. *Haven: The Unknown Story of 1,000 World War II Refugees.* New York: Coward-McCann, 1983.

Hirschmann, Ira. *Caution to the Winds.* New York: D. McKay Co., 1962.

Hoover, Herbert. *Proclamation 1872—Limiting the Immigration of Aliens into the United States on the Basis of National Origin, 1929.* The American Presidency Project Online. http://www.presidency.ucsb.edu

Long, Breckinridge, Memo to State Department Officials, 26 June 1940. Online by PBS, *America and the Holocaust.* www.pbs.org

———— *The War Diary of Breckinridge Long.* Lincoln, NE: University of Nebraska Press, 1966.

The United Nations War Crimes Commission. *History of the United Nations War Crimes Commission and the Laws of War.* London: His Majesty's Stationary Office, 1948.

U.S. House of Representatives. *Problems of World War II and Its Aftermath: Part 2, Selected Executive Session Hearings of the Committee, 1943–50.* Washington, DC, 1976.

Yasharoff, Norbert J. Interview by United States Holocaust Museum, 1989, transcript. United States Holocaust Museum Oral History Collection, Washington, DC.

Wallenberg, Raoul. *Raoul Wallenberg: Letters and Dispatches 1924–1944.* Translated by Kjersti Board. New York: Arcade Publishing, Inc., 1995.

Secondary Sources

Bates, Beth Tompkins. *Pullman Porters and the Rise of Protest Politics in Black America 1925–1945.* Chapel Hill: U. of North Carolina P., 2001.

Bauer, Yehuda. *A History of the Holocaust.* Danbury, CT: Franklin Watts, 1982.

———— *Rethinking the Holocaust.* New Haven, CT: Yale University Press, 2001.

Cook, Blanche Wiesen. *Eleanor Roosevelt: Volume One 1884–1933.* New York: Penguin Books, 1992.

Ehrenfreund, Norbert. *The Nuremberg Legacy.* New York: Palgrave Macmillan, 2007.

Feingold, Henry. *The Politics of Rescue*. New York: Waldon Press, Inc., 1970.

Friedman, Saul. *No Haven for the Oppressed*. Detroit: Wayne State University Press, 1973.

Gilbert, Martin. *Auschwitz and the Allies*. New York: Henry Holt and Co., 1981.

Goodwin, Doris. *No Ordinary Time*. New York: Simon & Schuster, Inc., 1994.

Kershaw, Alex. *The Envoy*. Cambridge, MA: Da Capo Press, 2010.

Medoff, Rafael. *Blowing the Whistle on Genocide*. West Lafayette, IN: Purdue University Press, 2009.

——— *FDR and the Holocaust: A Breach of Faith*. Washington, DC: The David Wyman Institute for Holocaust Studies, 2013.

Morse, Arthur D. *While Six Million Died*. Woodstock, NY: Ace Publishing Co., 1983.

Ostrow, Marty. *America and the Holocaust: Deceit and Indifference*. 60 min. PBS, 1993. Videocassette.

Robinson, Greg. *By Order of the President: FDR and the Internment of Japanese Americans*. Cambridge, MA: Harvard University Press, 2001.

Rosen, Robert. *Saving the Jews: Franklin D. Roosevelt and the Holocaust*. New York: Thunder's Mouth Press, 2006.

Tindall, George and David Shi, eds. *America: A Narrative History*. 4th ed, vol. 2. New York: W. W. Norton & Co., 1997.

United States Holocaust Memorial Museum. "Henry Morgenthau." *Holocaust Encyclopedia*. http://www.ushmm.org

Wyman, David. *A Race Against Death: Peter Bergson, America, and the Holocaust*. New York:, The New Press, 2002.

——— *The Abandonment of the Jews*. New York: The New Press, 1984.

ACKNOWLEDGMENTS

I AM GRATEFUL FOR THE opportunity to write about the extraordinary group of people who made up the War Refugee Board. They believed in the possibility of rescuing the Jews when few others did. It was an honor to spend time researching their efforts. America needs more passionate crusaders like John Pehle, Josiah DuBois, Henry Morgenthau, and the many others who represented the WRB across the world from 1944–45.

Thank you to everyone who made the process of creating my book so much easier for me, especially Robert Doran, Jane Dixon-Smith, and Kate Murphy.

This book could not have been written without the help and support of my former history professor, Dr. Leon Stein. He patiently saw this project through its many stages, from an idea for an undergraduate honors thesis to a book proposal to a finished manuscript. From the beginning he believed in my work and wisely told me to never give up. I am so grateful to have him as a mentor.

I also thank all of the libraries that generously shared the resources I needed, especially the Library of Congress, Penn State University, and the Franklin D. Roosevelt Presidential Library. Special thanks go to archivist Virginia Lewick from the FDR Library who worked tirelessly to track down documents I requested. In addition, I am grateful to the Schaumburg Township librarians who taught me to use the microfilm machine and answered my questions.

Last but not least, I thank my parents who put up with me through the ups and downs of writing and revising my manuscript. Thanks for your constant support and for giving me the frequent flyer miles so I could fly to New York for my research. I thank my dog Zoey for being a mostly patient companion while I typed, and for not eating any of my notes.

INDEX

Made in the USA
Lexington, KY
12 January 2016